The African Presence in the Bible

The African Presence in the Bible

Gospel Sermons
Rooted in History

William D. Watley
Raquel Annette St. Clair

Judson Press
Valley Forge

Library of Congress Cataloging-in-Publication Data
ISBN 0-8170-1349-0

Printed in the U.S.A.
06 05 04 03 02 01
10 9 8 7 6 5 4 3 2

Contents

Preface

by William D. Watley

"Reverend, are there any black people in the Bible?" I have been asked this question a number of times. It is essentially a question of relationship and identification. The Bible, the infallible written and revealed word of God, ministers most effectively to people when they see themselves in its pages and in its stories. That identification and relationship can be established existentially or ethnically or in terms of gender and other justice issues. For a people such as African Americans, who have been systemically excluded from much of the American psyche, ethnic as well as existential relationship with the Bible is important. For socially conscious African Americans whose oppression has been justified by the heretical and blasphemous "eisegesis" of the sacred texts, ethnic identification with the Scripture is critical for receptivity to the great eternal moral teachings of the Bible.

This book is designed to do two things. First, it establishes the truth of the African presence in the Scriptures in a positive and historically accurate manner. Second, it presents messages to address contemporary issues and situations for all people using the historical data of the presence of African peoples in the Scriptures.

In 1984 Dr. Samuel DeWitt Proctor consented to write a book with me that was published by Judson Press and entitled *Sermons from the Black Pulpit*. This is now my eleventh book. The association with Dr. Proctor in the writing of *Sermons from the Black Pulpit* that started me on my writing career has given my books a kind of instant audience and credibility that I would not have received as a fledgling author. Since a senior writer helped mentor me, I am pleased to be coauthoring this book with my young colleague, the Reverend Raquel St. Clair, executive minister at St. James A.M.E. Church. I predict a glorious ministry and bright future for this anointed, articulate, and Spirit-filled young woman in years to come.

I am grateful for the people of St. James whom I have served for the past fifteen years who continue to be a faithful and supportive church and an encouraging body of believers who have a love for God's Word. They make preaching easy. I am grateful to them for their patience and forbearance through the years. I am grateful to my wife, Muriel, for her faithfulness and endurance. I am appreciative to my administrative assistant, Sherri Schenck, and to Jean Graham for their typing assistance. My sister and friend Carolyn Scavella has served as the first reader and editor for every book I have written. This book is no exception. I am grateful to her for her perceptive editorial eye and her valuable comments.

Last but not least, I am grateful for the friendship, prayers, and loving counsel of another mentor, Dr. Elliott Mason, pastor emeritus and builder of the great Trinity Baptist Church in Los Angeles. He is a spiritual giant without peer and was a megachurch pastor before the popular usage of the term. He and Mother Mason are a powerful and unique team for the Lord. This book is dedicated to "Mom and Pop Mason."

It is my hope and prayer that the truth of Scripture told through the lives of the African people and their descendants found herein will be a lamp unto the feet and a light unto the paths of all those who read this book.

Preface

by Raquel Annette St. Clair

Dr. Watley and I first discussed the possibility of coauthoring a book in 1996. I was sitting in his office perusing a few of the sermon collections he had written, particularly *Preaching in Two Voices* and *Sermons from the Black Pulpit*, when he began to tell me how each book had come about. These three preachers — Dr. Samuel DeWitt Proctor, Suzan D. Johnson Cook, and Dr. William D. Watley himself — and their books intrigued me, because each one seemed to represent a new generation of preachers. The authorship of these books suggested a mentoring process and the passing of a preaching and publishing mantle. I questioned aloud, "Rev. Watley, would you ever consider writing a book with me?" My question was more theoretical than practical, like, "Do you think I can develop and preach sermons well enough for you to attach your name to mine?" His answer, as always, was more practice than theory, "Of course! Find a topic, and we'll develop a proposal and send it to my publisher."

During the course of that year and the next, the preaching and teaching at St. James focused on the subject of the African presence in the Bible. Much time and attention was given to this study, which was initially inspired by the publication of *The Original African Heritage Study Bible*. The purpose of our preaching and teaching for almost a year was not only to identify Africans, African lands, and people of African descent, but to preach the lessons of Christian discipleship they share. We wanted to move beyond "Who are they?" to answer the questions "What did they do?" and "How do they contribute to the faith?" It was an eye-opening experience that instilled a new level of appreciation, belonging, and cultural acceptance as we participated in telling the Christian story as a portion of our geographic, cultural, and religious heritage that began millennia before the slave trade. This, we decided, was to be the topic of our book.

There are many people to thank for this opportunity. First, I thank God for leading me to St. James and the mentoring of Dr. Watley. I thank Dr. Watley for agreeing to coauthor this book with me, for always seeing within me the potential for great things, and for refusing to allow me to settle for anything less. I thank him for the example of ministry and scholarship he has been and continues to be to me and am honored to call him my "father" in ministry.

I would also like to thank the people of St. James who have served as the original audience for these sermons. I am grateful for the privilege of preaching to and teaching such gracious people who have supported me as I have striven to work out ministry in their midst.

I am thankful to Rev. Alise Barrymore and Rev. Teresa Lynn Rushdan, my sister-friends and colleagues, for listening to many of these sermons before they were ready to be preached, identifying the wrinkles, and helping me to iron them out.

I am grateful to Geddes and Carrie Hanson, my seminary parents, for their love and encouragement. I am also grateful to the chair of my dissertation committee, Dr. Brian Blount, for his academic mentoring and support of my ministry to a local congregation from which works such as these are birthed.

I wish to especially thank two very important people who have shaped my life in more ways then they will ever know: my grandmother, Doretha Virginia St. Clair, who always told me, "Follow God. He's always made a way for you before," and my father, Barry L. St. Clair, who began telling me at the age of three, "Hold your head up. You are a strong, proud black woman." To them I dedicate this book.

1

We Are Included
Genesis 2:10–14

William D. Watley

A s an African American Christian, I must confess that there have been times when I have felt a sense of cultural and historical alienation from Christianity in general and the Bible in particular. When I read the Bible, I learn of the story of the Jews, or the people of Israel. I can understand and even relate to certain aspects of their history; however, since I am not Jewish, my ability to relate is limited. I read about the Promised Land or Palestine or Canaan in the Middle East, but I have no cultural ties or feelings of kinship to people who live in that part of the world. Thus, I have often found myself struggling to find myself culturally or historically in the Bible. Often I have felt that I had to force or try to fit my religious quest into somebody else's religious history and culture. Since the Bible does not tell the history of my people, at times I have felt like a second-class citizen. I have a feeling that I am not alone in my struggles and that a number of ethnically conscious and proud African Americans wrestle with the same kinds of issues.

Besides, with the rise of the Nation of Islam or with traditional Muslims or in the anger of a militant secular generation of young people, we often hear the statement that Christianity is a white man's religion. When we think about the complicity of white American Christianity with African American slavery and when we look at depictions in books and on television of biblical characters, such as Jesus, Moses, David, Bathsheba,

Mary, and other Israelites as whites, we don't have much of a defense. Our defense as Christians lies in our personal relationship with God, our love for Jesus, our baptism or anointing by the Holy Spirit, or our knowledge of black church history. Still there are times when in relation to the Bible we feel a sense of cultural and historical ambivalence, alienation, or anomie. In other words, at times we feel like either invisible people or "Johnny-come-latelies" to biblical history or salvation history.

When we read the Bible with educated understanding and an enlightened mind, however, we discover that we are neither invisible in the Scriptures nor late arrivals to salvation history. In the Book of Genesis, at the very beginning of the Bible, before we can get out of chapter 2, the presence of nonwhite people in general and African people in particular is established. Right after the creation of Adam and Eve, before the appearance of Satan in the Garden of Eden and the expulsion of the first humans from Paradise, the presence of African people is established in the Scriptures.

Genesis 2:8–9 speaks of the Garden of Eden, the first habitation of human beings. Verses 10–14 tell of a river with four branches that flowed from Eden — the Pishon, the Gihon, the Tigris, and the Euphrates. The location of the Pishon River is under dispute. Some scholars identify it as the branch of the Nile River known as the Blue Nile while other scholars locate it in Arabia. The Tigris and Euphrates Rivers begin in southeast Turkey and flow through Syria and Iraq and empty into the Persian Gulf. The Gihon is the branch of the Nile known as the White Nile. The Nile, at 4,160 miles long, is the world's longest river and is the only river in the world that flows from south to north. With its branches it flows through Egypt, the Sudan, and small areas of Ethiopia and Uganda.

We know that the Gihon is the Nile or the White Nile because the Bible says that it flowed around the whole land of Cush. Cush was the name given by the Egyptians to their neighbors to the south. The Hebrews also used this ancient Egyptian term. The Greeks used the term Ethiopians, which means "burnt faces" to refer to those black Africans that the Egyptians and Hebrews called Cushites. The Christians referred to these same black people as Nubians. The name Abyssinian refers to modern Ethiopians. It is a Muslim, Arabic, or Portuguese expression meaning "mixture" and refers to the combination of African and Arabic elements in Ethiopian culture. You will not find the name Africa in the Bible, because the Romans gave that name to the motherland after the Hebrew Scriptures had been compiled. The Romans named Africa after a Roman general who tried to conquer some of the northern tribes and failed.

Consequently, when the Bible refers to African people, it uses such terms as Egypt, Cush, Ethiopians, or Ham, who was one of Noah's sons and the father of Cush and Egypt. Thus, in Genesis 2:13 when the Gihon River that flows around the land of Cush is mentioned, the presence of African people is clearly established in the Bible. We may not know the exact location of the Garden of Eden, but we know this: it definitely was not anywhere near Europe. The four rivers indicate that it was located among the nonwhite, darker-skinned people who inhabited the African-Asiatic world. We may not know the exact location of Havilah, and there may be some conjecture about the Pishon River, but there is no doubt about the land of Cush and the river that flows around it.

Therefore, we do not have a Judeo-Christian heritage; we have an African Judeo-Christian heritage. Before Abraham, the spiritual father of the Jews, left the Ur of the Chaldees, the African presence in Scripture had not only been established, but Africans had begun to play an active role in shaping the biblical story. Thus, the biblical story cannot be told without the African presence. Persons who talk about our faith as a white people's religion don't know their Bible. Glenn Usry and Craig S. Keener have pointed out in their book *Black Man's Religion* that "more of the Bible is set in the region of northeast Asia than in Europe, even southern Europe; whereas Rome is mentioned twenty times and Greece twenty-six, Ethiopia appears forty times and Egypt over seven hundred...northern Europe no where appears in the Bible."[1]

Lest we forget, Nimrod, the son of Cush, was the first on

earth to become a mighty warrior (Genesis 10:8–9). He founded
Babel, where humans tried to build a tower to reach heaven.
Lest we forget, Abraham not only had a child by the African
woman Hagar, but he spent time in Africa. Lest we forget, Jacob
died in Africa. Lest we forget, Joseph had an Egyptian wife,
Moses had a Cushite wife, and Solomon had an Egyptian wife.
Lest we forget, most of Moses' life was spent in Egypt. Lest
we forget, it was a Cushite who brought David the news that
his son Absalom was dead. Lest we forget, the only queen to
ever visit Solomon was the queen of Sheba. Lest we forget, the
book known as the Song of Solomon was written in tribute to
a black woman. Lest we forget, the statement "I am black and
beautiful" was first uttered in Scripture (Song of Solomon 1:5).
Lest we forget, the psalmist has prophesied, "Princes shall come
out of Egypt; Ethiopia shall soon stretch out her hands unto
God" (Psalm 68:31, KJV). Lest we forget, whenever the kings of
Israel and Judah got into trouble, their first inclination was to
call on the pharaohs of Egypt to assist them. Lest we forget,
Jeremiah's life was saved by his Ethiopian friend, Ebed-melech.
Lest we forget, the prophet Zephaniah, who wrote the book
that bears his name, was a Cushite.

Lest we forget, when Herod was trying to destroy the baby
Jesus, an angel told Joseph and Mary to take him to Egypt. That
means that Jesus' early formative years were spent on African
soil. Lest we forget, when Jesus began to totter under the weight
of the cross, it was the black man Simon of Cyrene who helped
him carry his cross. Lest we forget, the first Gentile convert after
Pentecost was the Ethiopian eunuch. Lest we forget, Alexander
and Rufus, the sons of Simon of Cyrene, became leaders in the
early church. And when Paul sends them greetings, he refers to
their mother as his mother (Romans 16:13).

As African American Christians we are not afterthoughts.
We can easily find ourselves in the Scriptures. Others can leave
our contributions out of their history books and pretend that
we don't exist, but when we read our Bibles, we are included.

Not only are we included, we are also embraced. The Gihon
River flows around the whole land of Cush — not just part of

it. When I think about how the Gihon, or Nile, flows around the whole land of Cush, I am reminded of how God still opens wide arms of mercy and saves and embraces all of us. Likewise, the blood of Jesus encircles all of us and the Holy Spirit fills all of us when others would leave us out. It almost seems as if God looked into the future and saw how the children of Cush would be enslaved, mistreated, and abased and said, "The sin of humans may try to push them out, but when I cause my book to be written and the redemption story to be told, I'm going to find a way to write them in all through the script so that they will know that they belong to me."

It seems as if God said, "As the Gihon flows out of Eden, so my grace and greatness, my power and my peace, my salvation and my strength will flow into their lives. As the Nile is the longest river in the world, I will make their endurance long, their hopes and their vision long, for the difficult times that an insecure world puts them through. As the Nile is unique in that it is the only river that flows from south to north, I will give them unique gifts of song and sounds, of movement and music, of faith and feelings, of religion and rhythm among the people of the world."

As the Gihon embraces Cush, so some of us know that we have been embraced by God, who established us along the banks of the Gihon River. You ask how we have made it when human sin enslaved us for over four hundred years and then released us without even a token forty acres and a mule. The answer is that we have been embraced by God, who established us along the banks of the Gihon River. You ask how we make it when we are the last hired and the first fired. We have been embraced by God, who established us along the banks of the Gihon River. You ask how our women have been able to see visions, and our men have been able to dream dreams in the midst of nightmarish realities. The God who established us along the banks of the Gihon River has embraced us. You ask me how our children continue to believe in themselves when every message from the broader society is that they are nobodies. We have been embraced by the God who established us along the banks of the Gihon River.

You ask me how some of us have been able to get back up after life knocked us down. The same God who included us, also embraces us. When the world tried to break us up and mess us up, God who established us and Jesus who died for us, picked us up, fixed us up, and kept us up. As the Gihon River embraces Cush, underneath us have been everlasting arms. Thus, we could say with the hymn writer:

> What have I to dread, what have I to fear?
> Leaning on the everlasting arms?
> I have blessed peace with my Lord so dear,
> Leaning on the everlasting arms.[2]

Notes

1. Glenn Usry and Craig S. Keener, *Black Man's Religion* (Downers Grove, Ill.: Intervarsity Press, 1996), 75–76.
2. Elisha Hoffman, "Leaning on the Everlasting Arms."

2

There Is a Well for You
Genesis 21:8–19

Raquel Annette St. Clair

God is raising people of courage to do God's work. *God is doing the raising.* So we do not know who God will raise up or when or where. Actually, it doesn't matter. All that matters is that when God raises those men and women up, they do what God says.

Remember, we serve a God who has a way of inverting our expectations. God is a "first shall be last and last shall be first" kind of God — a God who will choose a shepherd boy to take the place of a mighty king, a God who will allow his Son to be born in a manger and then raise him to stoop no more. So do not think that the people God is raising up will look like, act like, or be like you expect.

God is raising up unexpected people from unexpected places, giving them unexpected promises, and sustaining them with unexpected provisions. God is raising people of courage to do God's work — people with a plan and a purpose, people who not only hear God's voice, but are faithful to God's call.

You see, Sarah is not the only person for whom God looks out and has plans. Sarah is not the only one God blesses. God also cares for Hagar. Yet in reading the biblical saga of Abraham, Sarah, Isaac, Hagar, and Ishmael, we have a tendency to read from Sarah's side even though this passage is Hagar's story, not Sarah's. Perhaps we read it from Sarah's side because we want to identify with her. Sarah — chosen by God, favored woman, mother of a nation, wife of a wealthy patriarch, and mistress of her household. Our identification with Sarah may not come from *being like* Sarah, but from *our desire to be like* Sarah. After all, as African Americans, we are "Aunt Hagar's children." But we all want to be favored rather than forsaken, accepted rather than rejected, wealthy rather than poor and struggling, an order giver rather than an order fulfiller. Yet this is exactly the position in which we find Hagar, the subject of our story. Maybe, just maybe, we read from Sarah's side because Hagar's position is too painfully close to the reality of our lives.

Hagar — slave to the desires of her ethnic, social, and economic "superior"; slave to the whims, desires, and decrees of another human being; slave to a woman named Sarah. Two women who might have found solidarity, commonality, and equality in another time or place where rich and poor, Israelite and Egyptian, could stand together, in this text were worlds apart. Hagar worked within the system by doing all she could to fulfill her role. From what we know, she had been an obedient servant. Because Hagar was Sarah's slave, Sarah didn't have to cook or clean or wash — Hagar did it all. And when Sarah grew impatient waiting on God, she insisted that Hagar bear her a child so that Sarah's husband could have an heir.

When Sarah finally conceived and bore Isaac, however, she no longer wanted that slave woman's child around. Why? Because she knew that Ishmael, as the firstborn son, was entitled to the larger share of Abraham's estate. How could the bondwoman's child inherit with the free woman's child? How could the poor woman's child receive the same as the rich woman's child? How could Ishmael be blessed along with Isaac? Sarah's answer was that these things could not be. Cast them out!

Do not think that because you are faithful everyone will like you or that because you are diligent everyone will receive you. Do not think that because you are hardworking everyone will accept you and that because you are loyal everyone will love you. These may be the exact reasons people do not want you around.

So Hagar is sent into the desert with a vessel of water and

some bread — insufficient provisions for the journey she has to make with her child. I often feel like Hagar — a "has not" in a world that has; being defined instead of defining myself; rejected because people do not think that I am their equal. I feel like I have a long way to go to reach my destination but do not have enough provisions for my journey.

You see, we have all been in the desert at one time or another. It's that place of loneliness and desperation, hopelessness and confusion, emptiness and fear, where the wind of the Spirit doesn't seem to blow, where there is no hiding place from the sun, where the provisions of God seem too far away. But even in the desert you can have comfort for your loneliness, hope for your hopelessness, and peace for your confusion. Even in the desert love can cast out every fear. Because even in the desert God is with you, and those who reject you cannot keep God from raising you up. In the desert God has provided a well, and those who do not support you cannot keep God from sustaining you. There is a well for you.

God is raising up people of courage from some unexpected places, and God has put his plan and purpose inside them. Your situation will not determine whether or not God will use you; your submission will. Your problem does not determine whether or not God will use you; your prayer power and perseverance will. Your brokenness will not determine whether or not God will use you; your belief in God will. The obstacles you face will not determine whether or not God will use you; your obedience to God will.

Just because you feel put out does not mean God cannot put you back in. Just because you feel down and out doesn't mean God cannot get you up and at 'em. We serve a God of resurrection power!

So maybe we have found ourselves in a desert, a place where it isn't easy to dream a dream or hold onto a vision or believe in a promise. But just because it isn't easy does not mean it is impossible. Too often we let go of the dream, the vision, the promise. We think that because we do not see the way out, there is no way out. We think that because we do not see how the need will be met, it will never be met. We think that because we do not know the answer or the solution, it cannot be found.

This is the arrogance of the faithless: If I did not see it, it did not happen. If I did not hear it, it was not said. If I did not touch it, it was not felt. If I do not think it is possible, it cannot be done. And because we cannot comprehend anything beyond our five senses, we never move beyond the present condition of our five senses. Proverbs 16:18 says, "Pride goes before destruction." The arrogance of the faithless means that we will continue to fall into the same mess we have been trying to get out of if we cannot look beyond ourselves and our situations to see God. If we are going to dream that dream, to hold onto that vision, to believe that promise, we must allow God to raise up and give us courage to press on. We do not have a God who is limited to our five senses but a faith-motivated God who enters into lives and who "calls into existence the things that do not exist" (Romans 4:17).

Beloved of God, hold on and don't let go of what God has given to you. For Hagar found out in her desert that her hopes and dreams did not have to die there, that circumstances do not outweigh God's power, that God's word is always the final word on any subject. The word of God came to Hagar saying, "Come, lift up the boy and hold him fast with your hand, for I will make a great nation of him" (Genesis 21:18). Notice that God said that *God* would do it.

"I will, not you, Hagar. Do not put your trust in yourself. I will, not you, Hagar. Don't look to others to insure your dream. I will, not you, Hagar. Don't you know that if I give the vision I will also give the provision?" In the same way, the word of God is coming to the people of God saying, "Come, people of God, lift up the promise, the needs, the brokenness, the heartache, the loneliness, and hold it fast in your hand, for *I will*. . . . I, not you, will fulfill my promises. I, not you, will meet the needs. I, not you, will mend the brokenness. I, not you, will heal the heartache. I, not you, will bring comfort into loneliness."

The reason we can trust God's "I will" is because we know that God is the great "I AM" in whatever desert we find ourselves.

What God has promised, God will perform. Whatever God has declared, God will deliver. Whatever God has begun, God will bring to completion. God has an "I AM" to silence every one of our "I am nots."

Yes, we struggle through the bad times and still hold fast to God's promises. And every need met by God, no matter how small and insignificant it may seem, is one step closer to the fulfillment of the promise. The reason I believe this is because before Ishmael could be made into a great nation, he first needed a drink of water. A drink of water may not seem like much when you think of the wilderness Hagar and Ishmael still had to cross. It may not seem like much when you think about the distance they still had to travel and about all the things that could go wrong. Yet a drink of water was enough to get them through the situation.

Too often we refuse the drink, refuse the well, refuse to take a leap of faith because the provision does not supply our every need at once. We allow the "what ifs" to paralyze us. What if this isn't enough to quench my thirst? What if we get thirsty later? What if this doesn't work? What if people talk about me? What if I can't pay next month's bills? What if...? What if...? What if...? We become so afraid that we would rather sit in the desert and die than rise up and accept the provision God puts before us. But Hagar took advantage of the opportunity God provided. She decided to believe God and trust that God's provision was enough. When God raised Hagar up, Hagar got up and did what God said to do.

Hagar, not God, had to walk to the well. Hagar, not God, had to give Ishmael a drink of water. Hagar, not God, had to continue living and doing by trusting in the faithfulness of God until the promise was fulfilled. Hagar walked to the well believing God's provision was enough. Hagar walked to the well so that they might live. And today God has a well for you. God is still in the business of raising people up out of impossible situations. God has a way of making a way out of no way at all. God has a way of turning nothing into something, nobodies into somebodies, and a little into much. This is the witness of Scripture.

I hear Moses affirming that God will lead you to a Promised Land and Joshua testifying that God will fight your battles along the way. David sang that God is a very present help in the time of trouble and that you can call on God night or day. God will go with you into a fiery furnace. God will be your wheel in the middle of a wheel. And if God can touch that woman with the issue of blood, there is nothing God can't heal. God is a way-maker, a burden bearer, a problem solver, and a prayer answerer. God is raising up a people of courage and providing for us in our desert places. There is a well for you. Will you walk to it?

3

Up from Egypt
Genesis 39

Raquel Annette St. Clair

> When Israel was in Egypt land, let my people go.
> Pressed so hard, they could not stand, let my people go.
> Go down Moses, way down in Egypt land.
> Tell ol' Pharaoh, "Let my people go!"
> — "Go Down Moses," slave song

The image set forth in "Go Down Moses" is the predominant picture many of us have of Egypt. When most people think about Egypt in the Bible, they think of the Hebrew slaves trying to gather enough straw to make bricks. They think of Egypt as a place of heavy oppression and hard taskmasters, a place where it took four hundred years, ten plagues, and a showdown at the Red Sea for God's people to be set free.

But that's not the whole story of Egypt in the Bible; that's only the Exodus story. Before there was an Exodus, there was a Genesis. And before there was a Moses, there was a Joseph. Perhaps we need to take a second look at Egypt, because Egypt's place in the Bible has not always been negative. Egypt is not only about being in bondage; it is also about believing until you get a breakthrough. Egypt is not only about blood, sweat, and tears; it is also about blessings, salvation, and triumph. Egypt is not only about disappointment that leads to despair; it is also about dedication that leads to deliverance.

Egypt isn't all positive; nor is it all negative. Egypt isn't all good; nor is it all bad. Egypt isn't all heaven, but it sure ain't

13

hell. Egypt is the real world, with real people, real problems, and real possibilities. Egypt isn't reserved for special folk; it is everybody's place, because we cannot get to where we are going without going through Egypt.

We can't go from Ethiopia, the place where we began, to Israel, the place where we belong, without going through Egypt. Abraham could not go from Ur of the Chaldees, the place of his past, to Canaan, the place of his promise, without going through Egypt. Jesus could not go from Bethlehem, the place of his birth, to Jerusalem, the place of his resurrection, without going through Egypt. And Joseph could not get from his father's pasture to Pharaoh's palace without going to Egypt.

It is Joseph's story that causes us to take a second look at Egypt. Even though we may sojourn there for longer than we would like, or we may not like how we got there, or we find ourselves outside the Promised Land, Joseph's story lets us know that in Egypt there is something for us and in Egypt God is with us. Sometimes we have to go through Egypt to see that God is with us. Sometimes the tables must turn in order to know that whatever blessings we receive come from God.

Joseph was the favored son of Jacob, the firstborn of Jacob's beloved wife Rachel. He didn't work in the fields or pasture the flock. No, he carried messages between his father's house and his brothers in the fields. He had the best clothes, the best chores, and the most love. And he was a spoiled tattletale who brought bad reports to his father about his brothers.

But in Egypt the tattletale had a tale told on him by Potiphar's wife. Then Joseph's fine clothes became tattered and dirty from years in prison. The favored son of Jacob became the rejected slave of no one.

The interesting thing is that the whole time Joseph is at home living a carefree life, God is nowhere mentioned in the text. But once Joseph is in Egypt, Genesis 39 tells us four times that "the LORD was with him" (vv. 2, 3, 21, 23), two times that "the LORD caused him to prosper" (vv. 3, 23), and one time that "the LORD blessed . . . for Joseph's sake" (v. 5). And every time he interpreted a dream, he gave the credit to God.

It's not that God wasn't with Joseph while he was home, but perhaps Joseph is like us. When we have achieved or have been given a certain status, when the blessings are coming so fast and troubles seem so far, when everything is looking up and going our way, there is nothing in our walk or our talk that points to praising God for all God has done. We are too busy enjoying the blessings, even taking credit for them — talking about *my* effort, *my* sacrifice, *my* hard work, or *my* idea. And if anyone were to write the story of our lives, there would be so much of us to write about that there would be no room to mention God.

Then trouble comes. We are no longer on top but are scraping the bottom. We are no longer part of the "in" crowd, because they have put us out. Nobody is helping us, and we cannot seem to help ourselves. Yet the blessings still come, the doors are still opened, and the prayers are still answered. We realize that God was with us every time we thought we were making it by ourselves, and God is with us every time we know we cannot make it on our own.

An Egypt experience teaches one to testify, "If it had not been the LORD who was on [my] side . . . " (Psalm 124:1). An Egypt experience causes one to say, "I need thee every hour."[1] An Egypt experience makes one sing, "He promised never to leave me, never to leave me alone."[2] For Egypt isn't just a place of hard times, but the place where one receives his or her healing.

There is some healing in Egypt because there were some hard times before you got there. Although Joseph was loved by his father, he was hated by his brothers. Although Joseph was favored by his father, he was rejected by his brothers. Although Joseph was special to his father, he was sold into slavery by his brothers.

There is some healing in Egypt because hard times do not end when you get there. Although Joseph was lifted up by Potiphar, he was lied on by Potiphar's wife. Although Joseph was favored by the prison guard, he was forgotten by the cup bearer and spent two more years in jail.

Joseph did not have to wait until he could leave Egypt to see God at work or for the situation to be turned around. God provided for Joseph in Egypt. In Egypt, Joseph married Asenath, the daughter of an Egyptian priest. Asenath bore Joseph two half African sons who would become two tribes of Israel and whose names testify to God's presence in Egypt. He named one son Manasseh, which means "making to forget," because God made him forget all of his hardships.

Egypt proves to us that only God can make us forget past pain — not a liquor bottle or drug needle; not a cigarette or another slice of cake; not more makeup, clothes, or jewelry; not even a new boyfriend or girlfriend. These things may ease the pain, but they will not erase it. They may cover the sorrow, but they will not cure it. They may hide the hurt, but they will not heal it. Joseph's pain did not go away when he left prison, received a job from Pharaoh, or gained the respect of Egypt. The pain and sorrow went away because God gave Joseph what he needed to let the past go. For the love of the father he lost, God gave him the love of a Pharaoh. For the coat of many colors that was torn and sprinkled with blood, God gave him fine linen clothes, a gold chain, and a signet ring. For the loneliness he must have felt in a foreign land, God gave him the love of a faithful African woman. Thus, when the second son was born, Joseph named him Ephraim, which means "to be fruitful," for God had made Joseph fruitful in the land of his misfortune.

Isn't that just like God — to do for us what we cannot do for ourselves, to turn sorrow into gladness, weeping into laughter, and misfortune into blessing? Isn't that just like God — to give hope in despair, strength in weakness, and comfort in confusion? And isn't that just like God — to lift us up when we are cast down, open his arms when others have pushed us away, give us love when we are lonely, and heal us when others leave us hurting?

Thanks be to God that we do not have to wait until we reach the Promised Land to get what we need. Egypt teaches us to say, "All that I've needed thy hand hath provided."[3] Egypt enables us to believe, "Weeping may linger for the night, but joy comes with the morning" (Psalm 30:5). Egypt causes us to testify, "Earth has no sorrow that Heaven cannot heal."[4] Egypt allows us to say, "If my mother and father forsake me, the LORD will take me up" (Psalm 27:10).

The last thing I want to tell you about Egypt is that Egypt isn't just a place of slavery; it is also a place of salvation. For seven years, Joseph saved grain in Egypt's storehouses. When famine came, Egypt was the only place that had food. Scripture says, "All the world came to Joseph in Egypt to buy grain" (Genesis 41:57). Not only was Egypt saved through the famine, but the rest of the world was saved because of Egypt.

When Israel had spent four hundred years in slavery in Egypt, Moses, who was born in Egypt, reared by Egyptians, educated in Egypt, and a prince in the court of Pharaoh, became the savior of Israel as he led them across the Red Sea. And when Herod sought to take Jesus' life and killed all the baby boys under two years old, Joseph and Mary took Jesus to Egypt, and Egypt's borders saved the Savior of the world.

Egypt shows us that salvation does not always happen in the places we expect, among the people we know, or in ways we can predict. Egypt shows us that salvation occurs when and where God acts, but most importantly, that it occurs for a purpose. God does not save us to stay in Egypt. God saves us to get us out of Egypt.

Abraham didn't stay in Egypt but left and kept on going to find a city whose founder and maker is God. Moses didn't stay in Egypt but left and kept on going until he met God on a mountaintop. Even Joseph didn't stay in Egypt, for when Israel left, they took Joseph's bones with them as they had promised. And Jesus didn't stay in Egypt either but left and kept on going until the people hung him high and stretched him wide, until he got up from a borrowed tomb and ascended to the right hand of God.

Egypt is the place we have to go through to see that God is with us. Egypt is the place we have to go through to allow God to heal us. Egypt is the place we have to go through to know that God can save us. Egypt is not our final destination, our end, or our goal.

Egypt teaches us to say, "Lord, I'm strivin', tryin' to make a hundred; ninety-nine and a half won't do."[5] Egypt enables us to say, "I'm going to work while I can, 'til I cannot work no more, while the blood is running warm in my veins."[6] Egypt allows us to say, "I'm pressing on the upward way. New heights I'm gaining every day. Still praying as I onward bound, Lord, plant my feet on higher ground."[7]

Notes

1. Annie Hawkes, "I Need Thee Every Hour."
2. Author unknown, "Never Alone."
3. Thomas Chrisholm, "Great Is Thy Faithfulness."
4. Thomas Moore, "Come, Ye Disconsolate."
5. Author unknown, "Ninety-nine and a Half Won't Do."
6. Negro spiritual, "While the Blood's Still Runnin' Warm in My Veins."
7. Johnson Oatman Jr., "Higher Ground."

4

Just Call Me Moses
Exodus 2:1-10

William D. Watley

I don't know if we have ever taken the time to think much about it, but in many ways a number of our lives parallel the life of Moses, the great Hebrew liberator, who is of African origin. To begin with, since he was born in Egypt, Moses was a native African who belonged to a Semite tribe known as the Hebrews. And as African Americans we are persons whose origin is Africa. Second, Moses was born to an oppressed people in the midst of a majority population, as are African Americans. Third, the Egyptians, another nonwhite people, were oppressing Moses' nonwhite Semite people. Although white racism is the defining element in the oppression of African Americans, we as African Americans also know the pain of having our own nonwhite sisters and brothers participate in our misery. Fourth, when Moses was born an edict of death for male Hebrew babies had been proclaimed in the land. African American men are still demonized — perceived by many to represent the devil incarnate — and they continue to be especially vulnerable to death at an early age. Fifth, Moses was a descendant of a mother named Jochebed, who refused to accept an edict of death for her child. Further, in an imaginative and determined way and being fortified by faith, she fought back to save her offspring. As African Americans we are descendants of those who refused to die but fought back that their children might have a better life.

Jochebed's plan was to save Moses in a basket on the Nile River. Moses' floating down the great Nile River is reminiscent of our lives during certain periods when we don't know where or how we will end up. Those of you who have read Steven Covey's *Seven Habits of Highly Effective People* will remember that one of his principles is to begin with the end in mind.[1] The problem with a lot of us is that we don't know what end we are to be working toward, and even if we knew, we don't feel as if we have much control. We don't know when or how this sickness, this period of sorrow, this season of suffering will end. We don't know where this relationship is headed or where our career is going. We don't know when or where the vision will become a reality. Like Moses in the basket, much of what is carrying us along is out of our control, so we float along not knowing what the end will be. What do we do when we have done all we know how to do and things are still out of control?

As the basket floated down the Nile, Miriam, Moses' sister, was watching from the shore, but she could only do so much. After all, the tide was carrying the basket. It's good to have loved ones and friends who watch out for us and who may even try to protect us, but we must always remember that human power can only do so much. Sometimes tides carry us — that is, some things happen to us that are beyond human control. Anyone who puts too much trust in another human being is bound to be disappointed, because no matter how much another may love us, what he or she can do for us has limits.

The basket floated down the Nile until it came to the place where Pharaoh's daughter chose to bathe. Isn't it interesting that the basket landed among the reeds at that very spot? When we look at the law of probability, the chances of a baby floating down the world's longest river and surviving are risky at best. Yet this basket not only reaches a safe landing, it lands at the very spot where Pharaoh's daughter of all people chose to bathe. For me there is only one explanation for this phenomenon: Someone besides Miriam was watching. Somebody bigger than Miriam, bigger than Jochebed, bigger than Pharaoh, and bigger than the Nile River was watching.

I once read a card that said, "God, the sea is so wide and my boat is so small." All of us can feel overwhelmed at times. During those times, however, we would do well to remember that the same God who holds the sea in the palm of his hand also watches over our little boats. The God who guided the little basket holding Moses along the Nile is able to bring us through choppy waters and storm-tossed seas to a place where statistics say we ought not be. When we consider where some of us started from and the circumstances under which we set sail and see where we landed, there's only one answer — God guided our little boats.

An old familiar story tells about a passenger ship at sea during a storm. The ship was being rocked furiously, and passengers were scurrying around in fear and panic. Some were even putting on life vests. Yet in the midst of all of this pandemonium a little boy sat calmly playing with his toys. One of the passengers noticed him and said, "Son, you had better put on a life vest or find a place of safety, because we are in great danger."

The boy looked up and said, "Mister, I'm not worried."

The passenger looked at the little boy in amazement and said, "Don't you hear the thunder and see the lightning? Don't you feel the rocking and reeling of the ship?"

The boy replied, "Yes, but I'm still not worried."

"Why?" asked the perplexed passenger.

The child looked up with a broad smile and in all faith said, "Because my daddy is the captain of the ship."

If we know that Jesus is our captain, we need not fear the sea no matter how small our boat. That's why Jesus could remain calm in a storm at sea. He knew that his Father held the sea. That's why Paul could remain calm in the storm recounted in Acts 27. He knew that no matter who had the title of "captain," his Savior was really in charge. We never have to fear the sea when we know who's in charge of it.

Not only did Moses' basket land at the right place, but Moses also did the right thing without his knowing it. Moses cried, and the heart of Pharaoh's daughter was touched. God not only watches over us, he also guides our actions. Sometimes we say or do the right thing that impresses or encourages or blesses others, and we don't know why what we said or did made such a lasting impression. That is God's Holy Spirit guiding us. Many times we are in situations not knowing what we are doing, just fumbling around trying to do the best we can. Sometimes others with more experience and better qualifications surround us. Yet to their surprise we manage to come upon the answer, leaving them to ask, "How did they do that?" Or "How did they come up with the answer?" That is the Holy Spirit guiding us. So when we find ourselves doing the right thing almost instinctively or to our own surprise, as well as to the surprise of others, we should not call it luck, but should say, "To God be the glory."

When Miriam saw that Pharaoh's daughter's heart was touched when she saw the baby Moses in the basket, she ran to her and said, " 'Shall I go and get you a nurse from the Hebrew women to nurse the child for you?' Pharaoh's daughter said to her, 'Yes.' So the girl went and called the child's mother. Pharaoh's daughter said to her, 'Take this child and nurse it for me, and I will give you your wages' " (Exodus 2:7–9). Miriam may not have been able to do much about the Nile River, but she was faithful to her task, because when God started moving, she still had a role to play. I know we can't do much about the Nile River that is carrying our loved ones, and we don't know where they will land. But if we are faithful in doing what we are supposed to do, when God begins to move, we will still have a role to play in their salvation, rescue, recovery, and resurrection.

According to the Scriptures, when Moses grew up, Jochebed brought him to Pharaoh's daughter, who took him as her son and named him Moses, because she said, "I drew him out of the water." We are like Moses, because all of us have been drawn out of something and lifted to something. Some of us, like Paul, have been drawn out of self-righteousness and lifted to serving and saving others. Some of us, like the prodigal son, have been drawn from a hog pen and lifted to self-dignity. Some of us, like Zacchaeus, have been drawn from greed to generosity. Some of us, like Peter, have been drawn from shame to salvation. Some of us, like Lazarus, have been drawn from death to deliverance. Some of us, like Legion, have been drawn from torment to testimony. Some of us, like the Samaritan woman, have been drawn from an object of gossip to a carrier of the gospel. Some of us, like John, have been drawn from temper to tenderness. Some of us, like Andrew, have been drawn from nobodiness to somebodiness. Some of us, like Thomas, have been drawn from doubt to devotion. Some of us, like Matthew, have been drawn from a disgraceful past to a delightful present. Some of us, like Mary Magdalene, have been drawn from loneliness to love. Some of us, like the widow with two mites, have been drawn from disregard to recognition and respect.

So when you see some people praising God with unrestrained zeal, don't call them emotional. Call them Moses, because they have been lifted. When you see others refusing to return evil for evil, don't call them foolish or naive. Call them Moses, because they have been lifted. When you see others recovering from what once had them bound, don't call them addicts or drunks. Call them Moses, because they have been lifted. When you see believers tithing and giving and giving, don't call them crazy. Call them Moses, because they have been lifted. When you see lives changed — when you see people spending more time in church, in prayer, and in studying God's Word — don't call them fanatics. Call them Moses, because they have been lifted.

That is what our faith is all about: Jesus coming into the world to do for us what Pharaoh's daughter tried to do for Moses — lift us. That is what Calvary is all about: Jesus doing for us what Pharaoh's daughter tried to do for Moses — lift us. That is what the resurrection is all about: Jesus doing for us what Pharaoh's daughter tried to do for Moses — lift us. That is what the second coming of Christ is all about: Jesus doing for us what Pharaoh's daughter tried to do for Moses — lift us. Just call us Moses, because we have been lifted.

In loving kindness Jesus came my soul in mercy to reclaim,
And from the depths of sin and shame through grace he
lifted me.
From sinking sand he lifted me; with tender hand he lifted me;
From shades of night to plains of light, O praise his name, he
lifted me![2]

Notes

1. Stephen R. Covey, *The Seven Habits of Highly Effective People* (New York: Simon and Schuster, 1989), 95–144.

2. Charles H. Gabriel, "He Lifted Me."

5

Jethro's Reminders
Exodus 18:1–12

Raquel Annette St. Clair

After the Lord led the children of Israel out of Egypt with a high hand, Jethro, Moses' father-in-law and priest of Midian, took Moses' first wife, Zipporah, and their two sons and met Moses and the newly freed Hebrews in Rephidim. Moses' Midianite wife, Zipporah, and father-in-law, Jethro, remind us of the African presence among the children of Israel. The land of Midian was located in the southern Arabian peninsula. The Midianites were a nomadic people who were traders. Although they occupied a land outside of Africa, in their early history the Midianites were identified with the Ishmaelites. Genesis 37:28, the story of Joseph being sold into slavery by his brothers, reads, "When some Midianite traders passed by, [Joseph's brothers] drew Joseph up, lifting him out of the pit, and sold him to the Ishmaelites for twenty pieces of silver. And they took Joseph to Egypt."

Remember that the Ishmaelites, who are interchangeable with the Midianites in this passage, are descendants of Abraham and Hagar — Sarah's Egyptian slave and Abraham's second wife (Genesis 16:3). Moses' Midianite wife and father-in-law further remind us that the children of Israel were not a homogeneous or pure people. They were racially, ethnically, nationally, and culturally mixed. The father of Israel, Abraham, first married a Chaldean. His second wife was Egyptian, and his third wife was Arabian. Joseph married an Egyptian woman, and his two half Egyptian sons, Ephraim and Manasseh, became two of the twelve tribes of Israel. Moses' first wife was an Arabian mixed with African blood. His second wife was a Cushite or Ethiopian woman, "for he had indeed married a Cushite woman" (Numbers 12:1).

And when the Israelites left Egypt, they traveled out with a group of people referred to as a "mixed crowd" (Exodus 12:38). It is therefore not surprising that people of the African diaspora — people of African descent outside the motherland — identify with the Israelites. For we are like them not only in our slavery and liberation, but also in our diversity as a people. African Americans, in the broad sense of the term — the United States is not the only "America" — are found in North America, Latin/Central America, South America, and the Caribbean. We, too, are nationally, culturally, ethnically, racially, and even linguistically mixed, speaking English, French, Spanish, Portuguese, and every dialect, variation, and mutation in between. And in the midst of such diversity, multiplicity, and plurality, there is a great danger of separatism, sectionalism, and division that causes people to see themselves as individuals rather than members of a community, because they focus on the little differences rather than on the overriding commonalties.

We, as African American men and women, allow differences to become divisions when differences in hair texture, style, and length; differences in skin color, eye color, and body proportions; differences in marital status, economic levels, and educational or employment achievements become good reasons to talk *about* somebody instead of talking *with* somebody.

As Christians we also allow differences to become divisions when differences in worship, liturgy, tradition, polity, dress, music, and doctrine keep us apart. We become divided when we will only worship in our denomination, with our tradition, with people who look like us. We become divided when we will only worship in our church, with our members, at our regular time. We become divided when someone looks at us the wrong way or says the wrong words. We become divided when someone gets caught doing the wrong thing (which, if the truth be told, is something we have done, are still doing, or think about doing) and we use it as an excuse to leave the church, thinking we can survive as a Christian all by ourselves. We may be members individually, but we are one body. We become divided when we concentrate on the little differences that divide us rather than the big God that unites us.

So every now and then, God sends a Jethro into our lives to remind us that although each of us is a child of God, each of us also belongs to the people of God. These two things form our Christian identity — not one or the other, but both together. And if we are to be a child of God who strengthens the people of God, Jethro reminds us that we have to get two things straight — our praise and our perspective.

When the Lord led the children of Israel across the Red Sea on dry land, news spread across the ancient near eastern desert from oasis to oasis like wildfire until it reached Jethro in Midian. The news was so big, the details so unbelievable, the story so sensational, that Jethro didn't wait for Moses to get to him. He packed up himself, his daughter, and his grandsons and went to hear the story firsthand from Moses. Some of us, however, are quick to run to hear about bad news or gossip. Then we complain about the division, cliquishness, and negativity in the church. Well, that is the way it is going to be if bad news is all we listen to and talk about, because bad news doesn't build community or promote unity, it breaks it down.

Jethro ran to hear the good news. God's Word is good news because it is "healing to the flesh" (Proverbs 4:22) and it "judges thoughts and intentions of the heart" (Hebrews 4:12). The joy of the Lord — not the mess someone brings — is my strength. When Jethro heard about all the Lord had done, he didn't turn up his nose, try to talk it down, try to find a rational explanation, or try to poke holes in Moses' story. He gave praise where praise was due. He rejoiced in what God had done, blessed God, and offered sacrifices.

Look at this: The Midianite praised God for what God did

for the Israelites. The priest of a foreign people who served foreign gods praised God for what God did for Moses and his people. A man who had never known slavery praised God for what God did for people who had endured four hundred years of slavery. A man who hadn't witnessed the devastation of ten plagues and hadn't been at the banks of the Red Sea praised God for what God did for a people who had escaped the plagues and walked through the sea on dry land. The Bible says that Jethro praised God for what God did for Moses, reminding us that praise doesn't have to have anything to do with us.

Praise is about God. It is not just about what God has done for me, but simply about what God has done — even if I wasn't there when it happened, if I didn't see it, if it didn't benefit me. If it wasn't my blessing or breakthrough, deliverance, healing, salvation, or sanctification; if God moved on behalf of someone else and I heard about it — Jethro reminds me that I ought to give God praise. Even if I can't call the recipients of God's blessings by name; if I don't know a thing about them; if we only have one person in common and that one person is Jesus — Jethro reminds me that I ought to give God praise. If someone gives a testimony, I ought to give thanks. If someone's prayer is answered, I ought to praise God. If God makes a way for someone, I ought to take time to worship.

Jethro reminds us that God's blessings are given to more than one person. So how dare we limit our praise to what God has done for one person. John writes, "For God so loved the world..." (John 3:16), not just you or me, but the whole world. We praise God for what God has done for me and what God has done for you.

If we offer praise to God for more than what God has done for us, including others' blessings, our attention moves to something higher, bigger, greater. We won't have time for pettiness, small-mindedness, or negativity. If we offer selfless praise to God, we will no longer think only of self, but also of others. We will see ourselves as a child of God and as part of the people of God. We will see ourselves as a Christian and as part of the Christian church. We will see ourselves as an individual member and as part of the body of Christ. We will not only believe, but will work together to belong.

Jethro further reminds us that if we give God selfless praise, we will gain a new perspective of who God is. After Moses' proclamation and Jethro's praise, Jethro said, "Now I know that the LORD is greater than all gods" (Exodus 18:11). It wasn't that Jethro didn't know about the Lord. Remember that Moses' burning bush experience occurred while tending Jethro's flocks in Midian. Jethro just had the Lord on the same level with all the other gods he knew about. Jethro was no different than some of us.

We keep God on the same level as our bills. If we thought God was greater, we would tithe consistently. We keep God on the same level as our friends. If we thought God was greater, we would talk to God before we got their advice or called the psychic hotline. We keep God on the same levels as our problems. If we thought God was greater, we would give God the praise and quit talking up the problem. We keep God on the same level as our families. We say we love them both, but we only spend time with our families on holidays, and we only spend time in the house of God on Christmas and Easter.

Sure Jethro knew about the Lord, but when he looked past his limited knowledge and experience with the Lord to see what the Lord had done for someone else, he got a glimpse of the Lord that expanded his previous understanding of who God is. All that God is, all that God can do, all that God has cannot be seen in one life. God is just too big. I can look at my own life and see a bit of who God is, a bit of what God can do, a bit of what God has.

I may know that God can be mother and father to a child who has lost her mother to heroin and whose father struggles with cancer, and say along with David, "If my father and mother forsake me, the LORD will take me up" (Psalm 27:10). I may know that my God can supply all my needs according to his riches in glory because God pays for my tuition, rent, car note, insurance, gas, electric, groceries, cable, phone, and clothes. He blesses me far above my deserving. I may know that God can open doors that others close; say yes when others say no, say now when others say not yet.

But if all I had was my life to look at, if all I knew was what God did for me, I'd never know that God could deliver someone from the bondage of drug and alcohol addiction. I'd never know that God could mend a heart broken by death or divorce. I'd never know that God could bring a prodigal son or daughter back home. I'd never know that God could help a single mother or father raise a child alone. I'd never know that God could open blinded eyes, unlock deaf ears, or loose mute tongues. I'd never know that God could multiply fish and loaves, cast out demons, heal incurable diseases, or raise the dead.

If all we had was our lives to look at, we would only know what God has done for us. But when we consider the witness of Scripture, when we hear the testimony of the saints, we know what God has done for them and we know of the infinite possibilities of what God can still do for us. God can answer prayer with fire from heaven like he did for Elijah. God can walk with you in a fiery furnace like he did for Shadrach, Meshach, and Abednego. God can protect you from enemies like he did David. Jesus can dry crying eyes like he did for Mary and Martha, give you living water like he did for the Samaritan woman, give you a second chance like he gave Peter, and remove your fears and doubts like he did for Thomas.

Jethro reminds us that when we look beyond ourselves and our individual experiences with God, we can say, "Now I know that the Lord is greater...." Greater than Ramses and the Red Sea, greater than Pharaoh and forced labor, greater than enslavement and Egyptians. We can say with our African American brothers and sisters, "Now I know that the Lord is greater...." Greater than slavery and segregation, greater than cross and church burnings, greater than discrimination and intimidation, greater than lynchings and layoffs. We can say with our Christian brothers and sisters, "Now I know that the Lord is greater...." Greater than every trial and tribulation, greater than every situation and circumstance, greater than every demon and disease, greater than every sin and shortcoming, greater than every problem and predicament, greater than every hurt and heartbreak.

When we look beyond ourselves, we can say with the songwriter, "How great thou art, How great thou art!"[1]

Note

1. Carl Boberg, "How Great Thou Art!"

6

When Trouble Erupts in Unexpected Places
Numbers 12:1-2

William D. Watley

The problem with evil is not simply that it causes trouble in our lives, but that often the trouble erupts in unexpected places. It arises in contexts and from persons, situations, sources, and even issues that we would least expect. The text of Numbers 12:1-2 is a case in point.

The journey of the Semitic tribe known as the Hebrews or Israelites from their enslavement in Egypt to Canaan, the land of promise, was fraught with trouble that erupted all along the way. Soon after their victory march out of Egypt, the Hebrews and the mixed multitude that came out of slavery with them discovered that Pharaoh's "Emancipation Proclamation," which came in the form of a command to get out of Egypt, was only the first step to their becoming a truly free, independent nation. On the way to their goal of a land of their own, they and their leader, Moses, ran into obstacle after obstacle that they were completely unprepared for mentally, emotionally, physically, and spiritually.

To begin with, the Israelites could not take the most direct route to the Promised Land because they would have had to march through the territories of the Philistines, who probably would have attacked. At this point in their journey they were not prepared to fight foes like the Philistines. Of course, it is a common rule of life that any effort to reach a goal often takes longer than we expect. Very few people reach their goals by following steps one, two, and three. More often than not, it takes steps one through ten to get where we want to go. More often than not, we end up taking the long way around to get to where we want to go. If you are a leader like Moses and you are trying to move people from a familiar past to an unfamiliar future that challenges them to go places they have never been before, expect the journey to take longer than you had calculated and expect to take the long way around.

Since the Israelites ended up going the long way, Pharaoh back in Egypt concluded that they had become lost in the desert and decided to go after them so that he could reenslave them. He caught up with them at a very vulnerable moment; they were at the banks of the Red Sea and surrounded by high mountains. When you are trying to go forward or do something worthwhile, expect what you are trying to outgrow or get away from to come after you in your vulnerable moments. Pharaohs never cease trying to recapture their slaves. Whether that pharaoh is called racism, sexism, an abusive past, guilt, fear, lust, lying, nicotine, alcohol, cocaine, or overeating — pharaohs always look for a vulnerable moment to recapture former slaves.

Because the journey to the Promised Land was taking longer than expected, the Israelites soon ran out of food. We, too, can expect some shortages on a long journey — shortages of faith, vision, endurance, and patience. Not only did they run out of bread, they also came to places where the water was bitter or where there was no water at all. On any journey to any place worthwhile, expect some bitter disappointments and bitter discouragement and setbacks. Sometimes people will present things to you that you just can't swallow. And at other times you will find yourself in a place of drought. You will pray and will receive no word from the Lord, no sign from the Spirit, no clue as to what you are to do. No inspiration to keep you going, no hiding place from pressure, just barrenness on the horizon and emptiness in your soul. Expect the drought that drains, where everything is going out and nothing seems to be coming in. But also expect that you will make it through, for God will step in and give you what you need to keep going step by step and day by day.

On a long journey expect some straying and forgetting. When Moses went up to Mount Sinai to commune with God and stayed longer than the Israelites felt was necessary, the people forgot who had brought them out of Egypt and began to worship a golden calf. On a long journey expect diversions that cloud the vision, along with some stumbling, occasional backsliding, doubting and straying, and some forgetting of who and whose we are and what we ought to be about. One would hope that we would be true no matter what. The truth, however, is that when things are taking longer than we thought, Satan will use delay as the opportunity to create doubt, confusion, and conflict within.

On their journey to the Promised Land, not only did the Israelites have to contend with a pharaoh who tried to re-capture them, but also an attack from the Amalekites, who simply decided to make an unprovoked war on the people of God as they moved to the place where God was taking them. On your journey expect new enemies to rise up and attack you without cause — either because of their own insecurities or because of jealousy and resentment over the ways you are being blessed.

In the midst of all the trouble that continued to erupt, Moses had to hear the constant whining, complaining, and nostalgia about how good slavery in Egypt had been. He even experi-enced occasional rebellion from those he was trying to lead. On a long journey when the going gets tough, expect the doubters, the visionless, the fainthearted, the weak in faith, the lazy who believe that the journey to the promised land ought not involve any sacrifice on their part, and the impatient who want things to happen right away to begin to blame leadership. They will com-plain about the inconvenience involved in pursuing something worthwhile. When the journey becomes long and difficult, ex-pect people to want to turn back and talk about how good it used to be. Expect rebellion from those who claim they could do it better.

As Moses led the Israelites through the wilderness, trouble erupted a number of times and in a variety of places. When we take the time to think about those instances and the persons and sources, we should not, however, be surprised. One could almost expect trouble to arise from those places and sources. Yet in Numbers 12 trouble arises for Moses from persons we never expect — Miriam and Aaron.

Surely not Miriam and Aaron. They were Moses' blood sister and brother. Surely not holy, sanctified, Spirit-filled, fire-baptized, tambourine-beating prophetess Miriam. Surely not Reverend, Doctor, Bishop, Archbishop, Cardinal, Moderator, Convention President Aaron, the head of the Levitical priesthood. Surely not Miriam, Moses' older sister, who had watched him as a baby floating down the Nile River in a basket and then had interceded when that basket had come to rest at the riverbank in the very spot where Pharaoh's daughter was bathing. Surely not Miriam, who had babysat, fed, and helped raise Moses. Surely not Aaron, whom God had given to Moses as a spokesperson when Moses went to Pharaoh with the command to let God's people go. Even though Aaron had come up shaky in the golden calf incident, that was years ago. Aaron had come over on the Lord's side and had been forgiven and restored to his position of leadership. Certainly after all this time Aaron had become settled and secure in his leadership and faith.

With all that the three of them had been through as a family and as leaders, surely at that point on their journey, Miriam and Aaron would not be creating trouble and causing confusion among the people. They had been as close as three fingers on a hand. Surely Miriam and Aaron would not be causing trouble for Moses. Tell me, preacher, that it just "ain't so."

Yes, in Numbers 12 trouble was erupting for Moses from Miriam and Aaron — the least likely source, the most unexpected place. And listen to the issue they were stirring up a mess over — Moses' Cushite wife. For the Bible is clear, Moses had "indeed married a Cushite woman." We remember who the Cushites were — they were the black African people who lived in sub-Sahara Africa to the south of Egypt. There is disagreement about Zipporah, Moses' first wife. Some scholars believe that she was more Semitic or Arabic than she was African. No doubt exists, however, about the ethnicity of Moses' second wife. She was a Cushite, a pure black African woman. Miriam and Aaron had problems with her, but not because she was black. After all, they were nonwhite themselves. Remember that Moses, Miriam, and Aaron were all born in Egypt and thus were native Africans. Perhaps they saw this Cushite sister as a threat to their position and prestige among the Israelites. Miriam, as a woman and Moses' big sister, probably felt most threatened by another woman in Moses' life. Miriam was probably the main instigator of the trouble, persuading her weaker brother, Aaron, who at times grew tired of living in Moses' shadow, to go along with her.

Hear Miriam and Aaron complain: "Has the Lord spoken only through Moses? Has he not spoken through us also?" Well, what does the Lord speaking to them have to do with Moses' Cushite wife? Even though Moses' African wife was the subject of the controversy, what Miriam and Aaron were really dealing with was a power play. When trouble erupts in unexpected places, often what people are fussing about is not really what they are fussing about. Often people lift up one thing when they are really upset about something deeper, something more sinister and not as obvious. Those of us who have had to deal with leaking roofs can tell you that sometimes where the stain appears on the wall or the ceiling is not where the leak is. Sometimes water has leaked into the roof from some other place and traveled to the spot where the stain appears. Sometimes the issue that is being discussed is not the real issue, and sometimes the person who is doing the talking is not the person who started the mess. Aaron may be out front throwing rocks, while Miriam is behind the scenes keeping him supplied with rocks and telling him where to throw them. While we concentrate on the rock throwers, we had better find out where they are getting their supply of rocks.

How did Moses handle this particular incidence of trouble that erupted from the unexpected source of Miriam and Aaron? First, let us note what Moses did not do. He did not blame his African wife whom God had blessed him with for his trouble. He did not reject his Cushite wife because of Miriam's and Aaron's problem with her. He did not become defensive. After all, he had done nothing wrong. He did not get into a fight with Miriam and Aaron. That would have done two things. First, it would have brought him down to their level. Second, it would have drained Moses of time, energy, and attention he needed for his continued leadership of the people. You can't get to where you are trying to go if you let messes sidetrack you. The purpose of a mess is to mess you up — mess up your mind so that you can't think right and mess up your spirit up so that you can't pray right, mess up your vision so that you can't see straight.

The Bible tells us that Moses was humble, more so than anyone on the face of the earth. Moses didn't even defend himself; he didn't even answer his critics. That's hard. You have to be mighty disciplined and secure and have great faith in God not to hit back when you're being hit at, particularly when those throwing the rocks are persons you would least suspect. Moses continued to be faithful and loving, to mind his business and do his job, and to keep focused on reaching the Promised Land.

Because of his faithfulness, Moses didn't have to fight his battles or answer his critics. God stepped in and did it for him. Numbers 12:4–9 says:

> Suddenly the LORD said to Moses, Aaron, and Miriam, "Come out you three, to the tent of meeting." So the LORD came down in a pillar of cloud, and stood at the entrance of the tent, and called Aaron and Miriam; and they both came forward. And he said, "Hear my words:
>
> > When there are prophets among you,
> > I the Lord make myself known to them in visions;
> > I speak to them in dreams.

> Not so with my servant Moses;
>> he is entrusted with all my house.
> With him I speak face to face —
>> clearly, not in riddles;
>> and he beholds the form of the LORD.

Why then were you not afraid to speak against my servant Moses?" And the anger of the Lord was kindled against them, and he departed.

Numbers 12:10–14 says:

> When the cloud went away from over the tent, Miriam had become leprous, as white as snow. And Aaron turned towards Miriam and saw that she was leprous. Then Aaron said to Moses, "Oh, my lord, do not punish us for a sin that we have so foolishly committed. Do not let her be like one stillborn, whose flesh is half consumed when it comes out of its mother's womb." And Moses cried to the LORD, "O God, please heal her." But the LORD said to Moses, "If her father had but spit in her face, would she not bear her shame for seven days? Let her be shut out of the camp for seven days, and after that she may be brought in again."

When troubles erupt in unexpected places, don't panic; pray. Don't fight; stay focused. Don't become sidetracked; continue to serve. Don't become disagreeable; stay disciplined. Don't get testy; just trust God to fight your battles and bring you through. God is still able to silence critics and faultfinders. God is still able to undo those who try to undercut you. He can give you victory over those who major in messes. If you are faithful, when trouble erupts in unexpected places, God will fight your battle, for the battle is not yours, but God's. God still intercedes for his children.

Jesus came into this world as captain of the Lord's host, and the Holy Spirit came as comfort and guide so that we might know that we are not alone when trouble erupts in unexpected places.

> For a child has been born for us,
>> a son given to us;

authority rests upon his shoulders;
and he is named
Wonderful Counselor, Mighty God,
Everlasting Father, Prince of Peace.
— Isaiah 9:6

If we have faith to trust God when trouble erupts in unexpected places, we will be able to say like Moses, "Arise, O LORD, let your enemies be scattered" (Numbers 10:35). Arise! Arise! Arise!

7

You Can Make It
Joshua 1:1–5

William D. Watley

We will make it in the new millennium. I do not know
what we will face, but I do know that we will make
it. How can I be so sure that nothing can stop us in the new
millennium? Because Joshua made it to the Promised Land. Let
us never forget that all of the slaves who originally left Egypt
died out during the forty-year sojourn in the wilderness with
the exception of two: Joshua of the tribe of Ephraim and Caleb
of the tribe of Judah. The Israelites who entered the Promised Land were the generation that was born and raised in the
wilderness. The only senior citizens in the group were Joshua
and Caleb. Caleb was special because he demonstrated that even
at age eighty-five one can still be active and vibrant, with forti-
tude and a future. Joshua is special because he was an Ephraimite. Who were the Ephraimites, and how do they relate to our theme
of the African presence in the Bible?

In Genesis 41 we are told that when Joseph rose to power
in Egypt, Pharaoh blessed him with an Egyptian wife named
Asenath. Of this union two children were born. The first
was Manasseh, which means forgetfulness, because Joseph said,
"God has made me forget all my hardship and all my father's house" (v. 51). The second was named Ephraim, which
means fruitfulness, because Joseph said, "God has made me
fruitful in the land of my misfortune" (v. 52). In Genesis
48 when Joseph's father Jacob was approaching death, he

elevated his two African grandchildren to the status of sons as were Joseph, Reuben, Simeon, and Judah. By elevating his grandsons to the rank of sons, Jacob made them direct recipients and inheritors of his estate. Although Ephraim was the younger of the two, Jacob also gave him more status than the older Manasseh.

Joshua was a descendant of Joseph and his African wife, Asenath. His tribe was not one of the original twelve tribes, but it had been positioned as a tribe or half tribe by the action of Jacob. Some may not have considered the Ephraimites pure Hebrews and not really a tribe since they were Jacob's grandchildren rather than his children. Yet no matter what others thought about Joshua and his people, when the Israelites marched into the Promised Land, Joshua was in the number. Not only was he one of the only two remaining slaves who had left Egypt to make it into the Promised Land, he was the leader of the Israelites. The one whose tribe may have been looked upon as the least and the last was the leader of the Israelites. The one whose tribe may have been looked down upon was chosen to succeed Moses, who died without entering the Promised Land. When the Book of Joshua opens, God's command to rise and conquer, God's promise of victory, and God's assurance of ever abiding companionship were given to Joshua, the one who was descended from an African woman.

If Joshua could make it to the Promised Land, we can make it in the new millennium. There may be some things about us, such as our race, our gender, or our past, that others may try to use against us. But if God is for us, then God is more than the world against us. If Joshua made it, we can make it also. Joshua made it for several reasons. First, he had a friend named Moses who mentored him. God will bring people to your life to be a blessing and to be your trusted friends. Sometimes you will wonder what you did to deserve them. They are God's gifts to you to help you in your time of need.

Sometimes a friend is someone like a Jonathan to David, who will strengthen your hand in the Lord. Sometimes that person is like the Ethiopian Ebed-melech to the prophet Jeremiah, who will intercede for you and rescue you out of the pit. Sometimes that person will be like a Ruth to Naomi, who will believe in you when you are so weighed down with sorrow that you can hardly believe in yourself. Sometimes that person will be like a Luke to Paul, someone you can always count on to do whatever needs to be done. Sometimes that person will be like a Jesus to Simon Peter, someone who will forgive you when you have messed up and give you another chance. Sometimes that person will be like a Mary Magdalene to Jesus, someone who will be there for you to do whatever he or she can when the world has crucified you and buried you. We can make it in the new millennium because God will send us the right person at the right time to help us make it. God has done it before, and God will do it again.

Joshua made it not only because God gave him a friend called Moses, but also because Joshua was faithful. Through all his forty years of wilderness wandering, his hardships and sacrifices, we never read of Joshua complaining. We read about the complaints of Moses' own brother and sister, Aaron and Miriam, but none from Joshua. We read about complaints of the masses of people but none from Joshua. We read about complaints of the spies that Moses sent out to survey the Promised Land but none from Joshua. We read about the complaints of Moses but none from Joshua. We further read of God's complaints about the Israelites' ingratitude, but we read of no complaints from Joshua. Through all the wilderness experiences, whenever Joshua is asked by Moses to do something, Joshua does it willingly. Because Joshua is so faithful, God rewards him by bringing him into the Promised Land as the leader of the Israelites.

We can make it in the new millennium if we are faithful to our vision, faithful to our principles, faithful to those whom God sends into our lives as blessings, faithful to our responsibilities — no matter how big or how small — and faithful to God. God still blesses and honors faithfulness. During the new millennium, like David, we will sin; like Elijah, we will feel overwhelmed; like John the Baptist, we may have questions; and like Peter, we will make mistakes; but if through it all God knows that we are trying to be faithful, God will take care of us.

> The steadfast love of the LORD never ceases,
>   his mercies never come to an end;
> they are new every morning;
>   great is thy faithfulness.
> — Lamentations 3:22–23

Joshua made it because God provided him a friend, because he was faithful, and also because he kept looking forward. When others wanted to turn back, Joshua kept looking forward. We can make it in the new millennium if we keep looking forward. No matter how frustrating the present or uncertain the future, keep looking forward. That is where God is calling us. Growth is forward. New heights and deeper depths are forward. Heaven is forward. We don't back into heaven; we go forward to heaven. Our bodies are designed for forward movement. Our feet face forward, and even though some of us act as if our heads are screwed on backward, our heads face forward.

Everything around us is facing forward. The computer industry is not talking about going back to the manual typewriter. Transportation is not talking about going back to the horse and buggy. As uncertain as the economy is, it is not talking about going back to the barter system. Medicine is not talking about going back to blood-letting. The housing industry is not talking about going back to building outhouses. The food industry is not talking about going back to the family farm. The only people I hear talking about going backward are church people. The only people I hear talking about "Take Me Back" and the "Old Time Religion" are God's people. No, if we want to make it in the new millennium, our thinking has to be forward.

Joshua made it because he had a friend, because he was faithful, because he kept looking forward, and because he was a fighter. He was able to follow Moses because he was a fighter. To make it in the new millennium we are going to have to fight our way through it. Sometimes we will fight on our feet, and sometimes we will fight on our knees. Sometimes we will fight with our hands, and sometimes we will fight with our heads. Sometimes we will fight standing our ground, and sometimes we will fight by retreating so that we can recoup our strength to fight again. Sometimes we will fight with the Word of God, and sometimes we will fight under the unction of the Holy Spirit. In any case, we will fight.

We don't accept the negativism of others as law and gospel; we fight back with faith. We don't accept bondage as irreversible and the rule of evil as inevitable; we fight back with courage and the name of Jesus. We fight ignorance with education, apathy with inspiration, and hatred with love. We fight failure with another try. We fight mountains by climbing them. We fight difficulties with endurance and delays with patience. We fight enemies with class. We fight lies with the truth. But we do not roll over and play dead or turn back or throw pity parties or allow the devil to gain the victory. We fight back. And Joshua proves that if we fight, we do not fight alone. "The LORD of hosts is with us; the God of Jacob is our refuge" (Psalm 46:7). Jesus Christ is our captain, and the Holy Spirit is our energizer.

If like Joshua we fight and keep looking forward and are faithful, God will give us friends, and then like Joshua we will be true Ephraimites, for Ephraim means "fruitful." Every place where the soles of our feet shall tread from the rising of the sun to the going down of the same shall be ours. No foe shall be able to stand against us all the days of our lives. As God was with Moses, as God was with Joshua, God will be with us. God shall neither fail us nor forsake us. We will be so fruitful that like another Joshua, whose name in Greek is Jesus, we can take the crosses that the world gives and use them as sources of blessing, means of victory, and the precursor to our resurrection and greatest hour. We will make it in the new millennium. Joshua the Ephraimite, though an inspiration, is dead. But Jesus the Christ is a living presence both now and forevermore.

How will we make it in the new millennium?

Take the name of Jesus with you, child of sorrow and of woe;
It will joy and comfort give you; take it then where'er you go.
Precious name, O how sweet! Hope of earth and joy of heaven;
Precious name, O how sweet! Hope of earth and joy of heaven.[1]

Note

1. Lydia Baxter, "Take the Name of Jesus with You."

8

The Cushite Messenger
2 Samuel 18:19–32

William D. Watley

When David's son Absalom was killed in battle, a Cushite was selected to carry the heartbreaking news to David. Who were the Cushites who are so frequently mentioned in the Bible? The term Cush was the name given by the Egyptians to their southern neighbors. The ancient Hebrews also used this Egyptian term to describe the people south of Egypt from the interior region of Africa. Instead of using the term Cush, the ancient Greeks gave them the name Ethiopia, which means "burnt faces." When Julian planted the Christian faith in sub-Sahara Africa in the sixth century A.D., he described the inhabitants of the region as Nubians. When Islam began its spread into this area around A.D. 700, the Muslims described the area with the Arabic term Bilad of Sudan, which means "land of the blacks." When the Europeans began to colonize Africa, they adopted the term Negro for the multiplicity of ebon-hued people they saw, which is a Spanish-Portuguese term coming from the Latin root *niger*, which means black.

Thus, the Cushites, Ethiopians, and Nubians are essentially the same people. The so-called Negro and the modern African American are descendants of this noble ancient people whose presence is so keenly felt in the Bible and whose influence is so widely spread in the world of the antiquities.

In 2 Samuel 18:21 the spotlight falls on a Cushite who was a member of David's private army. This Cushite may not have been the only African who fought with David. According to the eminent Old Testament African American scholar Dr. Charles Copher, "David's private army, of which the Cushite was a member was composed partially of Philistines who had come from Crete; and blacks from Ethiopia and Egypt were among the Cretan population, some as soldiers from early times."[1]

This Cushite was an independent soldier, not a slave. One of the great myths that has been circulated is that whenever we see black people in the Scriptures or read about them in ancient times, they were slaves or servants. Before the rise of color prejudice, the ancient blacks were held in high regard by the peoples of their times. The Greek historian Herodotus and Jewish historian Josephus speak glowingly of the ancient Ethiopians, referring to them as among the world's most beautiful people.

This Cushite soldier then was just that — a soldier — not a servant or a slave. At this point in his life, David was a deposed king and was running for his life. The individuals with David were those who chose to be with him. The Cushite chose David over Absalom. Thus, he was devoted at a time when David's own son and many of his trusted counselors and supposedly loyal followers had betrayed David.

Not only was this Cushite devoted, he was also dutiful. The Cushite had to carry an unpleasant message, one that would deeply grieve the king to whom he had chosen to be devoted. But carry the message he did, because it was his duty. That's what duty is all about: doing what we are supposed to do even when we would prefer that someone else do it. Someone else, however, was not assigned our duty, so we must dutifully do the difficult.

Not only was the Cushite messenger devoted and dutiful, he was also dependable. A message such as the one he was to carry could not be entrusted to just anyone. One was needed who was diligent in carrying the message and who would give the right message the right way. David's general, Joab, selected the Cushite because he knew he could depend on him to diligently carry the message in the right way.

The Cushite was devoted, dutiful, dependable, and determined. As he was running, Ahimaaz, another messenger, overtook him and passed him. The Cushite, however, continued to run with his message. He was determined to take his message to the king though others were ahead of him. It is a good thing the Cushite was determined to carry his message, because when Ahimaaz reached the king, he had nothing to say. He was just running to be running. If the Cushite had quit running because someone else was ahead of him, David would not have received the message he needed to hear. But because the Cushite was determined and kept running, he was able to reach his goal and deliver the message himself in his way to the king.

Let us never forget that we as latter-day Cushites have a message to deliver. We have a message that African American men who are still the most suspect, feared, misunderstood, falsely accused, and vulnerable males of this society need to hear. We have a message that African American men need to hear lest we tragically build a fragile manhood on the continued domination and oppression of women, mimicking the sinful sexism of majority men. We have a message that African American women who bear the double burden of sexism and racism and are sometimes in triple jeopardy — poverty, sexism, and racism — need to hear.

We have the message of Richard Allen, who believed in self-help. We have the message of Henry McNeal Turner: God is on the side of the oppressed. We have the message of Daniel Payne: We need a prepared head as well as a warm heart. We have the message of William Paul Quinn: We can dare to face new frontiers. We have the message of Nat Turner: It is better to die fighting for freedom than to live as a slave. We have the message of Harriet Tubman: Don't forget to reach back for your brother and sister still in bondage. We have the message of Sojourner Truth: Let no one look down on you. We have the message of Benjamin Banneker: Genius is no respecter of color. We have the message of Booker T. Washington: Cast down your buckets where you are. We have the message of Marcus Garvey: We are a mighty people. We have the message of Rosa Parks: We can start a revolution if we don't move from our beliefs. We have the message of Shirley Chisholm: We can be "unbought and unbossed." We have the message of James Weldon Johnson: We can sing a song full of the faith that the dark past has taught us. We have the message of Mahalia Jackson: He's got the whole world in his hands. We have the message of Mary McCleod Bethune: Strive for excellence. We have the message of Malcolm X: Fear no man or woman. We have the message of Martin Luther King: We will get to the promised land.

As God's redeemed children, we have a message to carry — a true message that we won't have to retract. It is a message that will not degrade any community or deprive any people. It is a message of hope and not hate, love and not lies, salvation and not smut, deliverance and not division, reconciliation and not rejection, help and not hindrance, restoration and not racism, honesty and not hypocrisy, sincerity and not showmanship. It is a message about God's delivering power, Jesus' cleansing power, and the Holy Spirit's keeping power. It is a story of a God who so loved the world that he gave his only begotten Son that whosoever believes on him shall not perish but have everlasting life. It is a story of Jesus, who said:

> "The Spirit of the Lord is upon me,
>   because he has anointed me
>   to bring good news to the poor.
> He has sent me to proclaim release to the captives
>   and recovery of sight to the blind,
>   to let the oppressed go free,
> to proclaim the year of the Lord's favor."
> — Luke 4:18–19

It is a story of the Holy Spirit who gives us fruit to sustain us and gifts for service. It is a story about the devil's defeat and death's demise. It is a story about transforming and being transformed where we are as we await the coming of a new heaven and a new earth. It is a story about a God who keeps promises and a Bible whose truth endures to all generations. We have a message that this world needs to hear.

To give this message, however, we have to be devoted — devoted to the God who has brought us to this place; devoted to

Christ who has saved us; devoted to the Holy Spirit, who has filled us; devoted to the Bible that has guided us; devoted to the faith that has kept us; devoted to the church that has nourished us; devoted to leadership that has served us; devoted to the principles that have inspired us; devoted to each other as we help each other bear our burdens; devoted to others who have supported us; devoted to the kingdom of God, which frees us. We have to be devoted.

Not only must we be devoted, we must also be dutiful. Sometimes we have to serve when we would rather relax, stand when we would rather stoop, go when we would rather stay, run when we would rather rest, speak when we would rather be silent, become involved when we would rather be inactive. But we know what we promised the Lord; we know what the Lord called us to do. D U T Y — doing usefully through years. Duty is not something we do when it is convenient or easy. It is doing usefully, making our contribution through the years, in season and out of season, through praise and criticism, through good times and bad times.

Where would we be if others before us hadn't done their duty? Jesus did his duty as a Son, and we saw the heavenly Father in him. He did his duty as a Savior, and we have been redeemed. He did his duty as a friend, and we received another chance. He did his duty as a teacher, and we received the Sermon on the Mount.

Not only must we be devoted and dutiful; we must also be dependable. How dependable are we? How dependable is our faith? Will any rumor or trial cause us to doubt? How dependable is our love? Are our affections as fickle as political expediency? How dependable is our word? Do we break it as easily as we give it? How dependable is our commitment? Are we fair weather runners? How dependable is our friendship? Do we forsake them when it becomes inconvenient?

God needs dependable people — people like Daniel who won't stop praying even in a lion's den; people like the three Hebrew boys who won't bow even if it means being cast into a fiery furnace; people like John the Baptist who love nothing but truth and hate nothing but sin; people like Paul who keep on working even when thorns in the flesh won't go away; people like John the Revelator who stand in banishment and still see the glory of God; people like Jesus whose love, devotion, duty, and dependability Calvary can't kill.

Like the Cushite messenger, to bring the message to our destination we must not only be devoted, dutiful, and dependable, we must also be determined. Sometimes we may get discouraged because others seem to be outrunning us or are ahead of us. That's all right. If you have a message to tell, a story to share, a testimony to give, a song to sing, a service to render — keep on running. Over high hills and through deep valleys, though headwinds are against you and hellhounds are upon you, keep running. When nobody else is around to encourage you, keep running.

Keep running, because the message and the mission were given to you; though others run ahead, they can't tell your message like you can. Keep running with determination, because the King waits to hear from you. That's why in the final analysis we keep running: We know that the King stands at the finish line, and we want to give our report. We don't know everybody who will be there to greet us when we come to the end of our journey, but we know "one somebody" who will be there — the King.

That is why we keep serving without thanks or recognition. That is why we keep being dutiful when we are talked about and falsely accused. We know that at the end of the journey the King awaits to hear what we have to say. The Cushite in our text ran to King David, but we are running to see Jesus Christ, King of Kings and Lord of Lords. And he shall reign forever and ever and ever. Hallelujah!

Note

1. Charles Copher, "The Black Presence in the Old Testament," in *Stony the Road We Trod*, Cain Hope Felder, ed. (Minneapolis: Fortress Press, 1991), 157–58.

9

Ships That Never Sailed
1 Kings 22:48

William D. Watley

First Kings 22:48 tells us of the ill-fated plans of King Jehoshaphat to send ships to Africa for gold. To refresh our
memory, Ezion-geber, the place from which the ships were to
have set sail, was the main seaport of ancient Palestine. Their
destination was to have been Ophir, which was located in East
Africa in the vicinity of Somaliland. In biblical times Ophir
would probably have been either a part of or an extension of
the Ethiopian empire, which ranged into southern Arabia. In
the ancient biblical world, the gold of Ophir was the best to be
found anywhere. There are a number of references to the gold
of Ophir in the Hebrew Scriptures (e.g., Job 22:24; 28:12–16;
Psalm 45:9; Isaiah 13:12) and in the apocryphal book of Sirach (7:18). Each reference alludes to the fine quality of the gold
of Ophir.

Jehoshaphat was not the first Jewish king to send ships to
Ophir for gold. In 1 Kings 9 and 10 we are told that Solomon
sent a fleet of ships to Ophir for gold. And in 1 Chronicles 29:4
we are told that before Solomon, his father David personally
owned great quantities of gold from Ophir. First Kings 22:48,
however, tells us that the plans of King Jehoshaphat to send ships
to Africa to bring back gold were not realized because the fleet
that he built was shipwrecked even before it set sail from Ezion-
geber. Jehoshaphat faced the reality of building ships that never
set sail.

That is the reality that a number of us have faced or will face — building ships that never set sail. When we see children who are dying from AIDS, we often are observing ships that will never set sail. When we attend the funerals of young people, we are looking at ships that never sailed. When we look at broken relationships and realize that what ended them was not a major crisis but old issues that were never resolved because we vainly hoped they would work themselves out over time, we often are observing ships that never sailed. Very few things work themselves out over time; people usually work things out over time. When a relationship erupts because of what we didn't work out before we consummated it in marriage or in bed, we look back and realize that the relationship was shipwrecked before it left the harbor. And although it was in the water, it was not sailing anywhere.

When we look at lives that have gone nowhere and the potential that has gone unrealized, we are looking at ships that never sailed. When we look at people who could become powerful witnesses in the kingdom of God but who are quickly turned off by gossip, pettiness, church politics, and the imperfections of others, we are looking at ships that never sailed. Any long-time believers whose claim to fame is that "I've been here," are ships that never sailed. They are just in the water at port. They never left Ezion-geber; they never grew deeper in the Lord. Fear of the new, complacency, and sometimes ignorance have shipwrecked them.

Jehoshaphat's ships never set sail, not because something was structurally wrong with them, but because they were wrecked in the port. We might as well try to make something out of our lives, because we are going to have trouble whether we are trying to be something or not. Sometimes we believe that if we just go along quietly, mind our own business, don't create any waves, don't rock the boat, that problems will pass us by and trouble will blow over us. Jehoshaphat's experience, however, demonstrates that storms and misfortune not only attack ships on the high seas that are trying to go somewhere, but also attack ships in port that are doing nothing. Since people are going to talk about us, they might as well talk about the fact that we are trying to be something rather than going nowhere. Since we're going to have trouble anyway, let's have some while we are working rather than stand around doing nothing. I'm not a great football fan, but I know this much: It is harder to tackle someone who is running at full speed than someone who is standing still. Since we are going to have storms anyway, let's have them while we are in the Lord, in God's Word, in God's service, and in prayer rather than relying on our own strength and the security and comfort of our own port.

I do not know why Jehoshaphat's ships were wrecked at Ezion-geber, but I do know that Jehoshaphat did not lie down and die or abandon the throne because his ships were wrecked. Life for him went on even with wrecked ships. We do not know why some ships never set sail anymore than we can explain how a bumblebee whose body is too heavy to support its wing structure is able to fly, or how a grotesque, creeping caterpillar becomes a graceful butterfly, or how a black and brown seed produces a watermelon that is red on the inside, green on the outside, with a white rind in between. We just don't have answers for some things in life. When our plans are shipwrecked before they leave port, when ships that appear so seaworthy never set sail, we can spend all of our time asking why and being brokenhearted and bitter, yet never come up with the answer. Or like Jehoshaphat, we can understand that life has to go on for us, wrecked ships or not. The ships may be gone, but we are still here clothed in our right mind with a reasonable portion of health and strength.

When life has to go on after the ships that we built with great hopes never set sail, it is good to know God. Some people try to face life after shipwrecked plans without God, but personally I'm glad that I don't have to rely on my own strength and smarts. Jehoshaphat was not a perfect king, but he knew how to seek the Lord. In 1 Kings 22 when Ahab of Israel sought Jehoshaphat's help in making war on Syria to recapture the city of Ramoth in Gilead, Jehoshaphat insisted they inquire of the Lord before going into battle. And he would not stop his inquiries until he was sure that he had received a true word from heaven.

When we know God, we receive the assurance that we will be supplied with whatever we need to face life after shipwrecked plans. When we think about how God equips a little honeybee to deal with its world, then we can rest assured that God will help us handle ours. As small as a honeybee's brain is, it is still able to organize a honeycomb city consisting of ten thousand cells for honey; twelve thousand cells for larvae, and private quarters for the queen. When temperatures rise and it seems as if the wax may melt and the honey be lost, the bees organize themselves into squads, put sentinels at the entrance, glue their feet down, and then, with flapping wings, create a ventilation system that puts a fan to shame. It is amazing that the small bee's brain is able to oversee the flowers in a twenty-square-mile radius.[1] If God is able to equip a small bee's brain to do all of that, then we ought to know that God will give us whatever we need to keep on going when the ships we built to take us to new places never set sail.

When ships don't sail, remember that life goes on and that God will give us whatever we need to face all of our tomorrows without today's ships. Also remember that there is still meaning and purpose to life and that everybody has some ships in their lives that don't sail. Moses expected to personally lead the children of Israel into the Promised Land, but that ship never sailed. Centuries later, however, when our Lord Jesus was transfigured on Mount Hermon, Moses stepped across the barriers of time and stood with him. David wanted to build a temple. That ship didn't sail. But he laid the groundwork for his son Solomon to build it. John the Baptist expected a messiah of wrath and judgment. That ship didn't sail. Instead, Jesus told his disciples, "Go and tell John what you hear and see: the blind receive their sight, the lame walk, the lepers are cleansed, the deaf hear, the dead are raised, and the poor have good news brought to them. And blessed is anyone who takes no offense at me" (Matthew 11:4–6).

The disciples expected Jesus to establish an earthly throne. When he was crucified, all their plans were shipwrecked in the port of Ezion-geber called Calvary. But early Sunday morning Jesus rose to declare, "All authority in heaven and on earth has been given to me" (Matthew 28:18). Paul expected Jesus to return during his lifetime. That ship did not sail. But hear Paul's testimony, "I have fought the good fight, I have finished the race, I have kept the faith. From now on there is reserved for me the crown of righteousness, which the Lord, the righteous judge, will give me on that day, and not only to me but also to all who have longed for his appearing" (2 Timothy 4:7–8). The writer of Hebrews listed a number of Old Testament saints and then declared, "All of these died in faith without having received the promises, but from a distance they saw and greeted them.... Therefore God is not ashamed to be called their God; indeed, he has prepared a city for them" (11:13–16).

When ships never sail, remember that life must go on, that God will prepare us for it, that life still has meaning and purpose. Don't ever forget that God cares for us. I don't know why some plans are shipwrecked. I don't know why some of our most cherished dreams and noble aspirations never leave port and never set sail. But I do know that through it all God has never taken his hands off our lives, God still holds us. That is why we didn't go down with our ships and that is why we are equipped to face our tomorrows. I'm like the poet:

I know not where the islands lift their fronded palms in air —
I only know I cannot drift beyond His love and care.[2]

When ships don't sail, when storms wreck them as they are anchored at Ezion-geber, remember that you have a Savior who will stand by you when the storms of life are raging. I have had some ships that didn't sail, and I am a personal witness that when ships don't sail, God will take care of us.

Notes

1. Lee Tan, *7700 Illustrations* (Rockville, Md.: Assurance Publishers, 1982), 612, no. 2514.

2. John Greenleaf Whittier, "The Eternal Goodness."

10

A Message of Love
Song of Solomon 5:2–8

Raquel Annette St. Clair

The Song of Solomon is the most sensual, seductive, and therefore most shocking book in the Bible. It distinguishes itself with its unapologetic, unashamed, uncompromising descriptions of love, nature, and the nature of love. Moreover, the book that we know as the Song of Solomon is true to its Hebrew name. It is indeed a *šîr hašîrîm* (pronounced, "sheer hasheereem"), "The Song of Many Songs," "The Most Excellent/Most Superlative Song," because past and present love songs and poetry don't compare.

Elizabeth Barrett Browning asked, "How do I love thee? / Let me count the ways."[1] And the woman in the Song of Solomon does count the ways:

> My beloved is all radiant and ruddy,
>   distinguished among ten thousand.
> His head is the finest gold;
>   his locks are wavy,
>   black as a raven.
> His eyes are like doves
>   beside springs of water,
> bathed in milk,
>   fitly set.
> His cheeks are like beds of spices,
>   yielding fragrance.

> His lips are lilies,
>   distilling liquid myrrh.
> His arms are rounded gold,
>   set with jewels.
> His body is ivory work,
>   encrusted with sapphires.
> His legs are alabaster columns,
>   set upon bases of gold.
> His appearance is like Lebanon,
>   choice as the cedars.
> His speech is most sweet,
>   and he is altogether desirable.
> This is my beloved and this is my friend,
>   O daughters of Jerusalem.
> —5:10–16

Lord Byron said, "She walks in beauty, like the night. / Of cloudless climes and starry skies; / And all that's best of dark and bright / meet in her aspect and her eyes."[2] While the Song of Solomon puts it simply:

> You have ravished my heart, my sister, my bride.
>   you have ravished my heart with a glance of your eyes
> — 4:9

Diana Ross sang, "You can't hurry love; you just have to wait." The woman in the Song of Solomon goes one step further:

> I adjure, O daughters of Jerusalem,
>   by the gazelles and the wild does:
> do not stir up or awaken love
>   until it is ready.
> — 2:7

King Floyd said, "Groove me," but the message of this book is "Woo me."

Yet with all of its truth and beauty, the Song of Solomon has been one of the most difficult biblical books to explain, rarely read or preached from the pulpit, and in some churches even removed from the Bibles in the pews. Even we modern-day Christians are uncomfortable with its candid description of human sexuality, embarrassed by its praise of the human body, and ill at ease with its expressions of human desire. Perhaps this book is difficult to integrate into a Christian mentality because we get so caught up in the details, descriptions, and declarations on the surface that we miss the true substance that gives the surface its meaning.

What makes the Song of Solomon distinctive is more than literary style — genre, meter, and tone. It is more than the only book in which a female speaks through her own unmediated voice. It is more than this same woman being of African descent[3] and boldly declaring, "I am black and beautiful" (1:5). It is more than the impressive parallels with ancient Egyptian love poetry.[4] It isn't even the subject matter — love, because the subject of all sixty-six books of the Bible is the loving acts of a loving God who by John's definition is love.

Therefore, it is my humble opinion that the central factor that distinguishes the Song of Solomon from the other sixty-five books in the Bible is found in the qualitative difference between loving and being in love. Love will make you patient and persevering. Being in love will add some passion to your persistence. Love will inspire dedication. Being in love will add desire to your devotion. Love is defined as eternal. Being in love means spending that time extravagantly, because love will make you give, but being in love can make you give what you do not have and buy what you cannot afford.

The difference between loving and being in love is the difference between the steady tone of 1 Corinthians 13 and the intense highs and lows of the third chapter of the Song of Solomon. The difference between loving and being in love is the difference between Paul's statement that "love never ends" (1 Corinthians 13:8) and the Songs of Solomon's exclamation that

> love is strong as death,
>   passion as fierce as the grave.
> Its flashes are flashes of fire,
>   a raging flame.
>
>   — 8:6

The difference between loving and being in love is the difference between 1 John's analogy of love as light and the Song of Solomon's description of love as fire.

And as Christians, we have become more spiritually comfortable when speaking of the former — loving — especially when it comes to God. We know that God is love, that God so loved the world, that Jesus loves me. We know that God's love is patient, persevering, dedicated, never ends, and is the light that removes all darkness. But have we ever considered that God is in love? That God's love is also persistent, passionate, and full of desire? That God's love is not only light but also a fire that "many waters cannot quench" (Song of Solomon 8:7)? The Song of Solomon is not only a love song between two lovesick human beings; the Christian church has for centuries read it as a lovesick God's love song to creation and a lovesick Christ's love song to the church. The testimony of Scripture is that not only does God love us, but everything God does shows that God is in love with us too. God is like the black woman in the Song of Solomon. Take for example 5:2–5.

The woman is in bed when her beloved knocks at the door. There is no doubt that she loves him, because the poem says that even though she was asleep her heart was awake. Yet two concerns come to her mind: I am already undressed and really do not feel like getting dressed. I am already bathed and don't want to get my feet dirty answering the door. In other words, she had already washed her makeup off, put her beauty mask on, and put her curlers in, and here he comes knocking at the door.

The issue isn't whether or not she loves him. The issue is whether she has enough desire for him, enough "I can't wait to see you in the morning; I've got to get up now" kind of love that will make her leave behind the comfort of her bed, the convenience of her night clothes, and the cleansing of her bath. Enough to become uncomfortable so that he can get out of the night, out of the cold, and into the shelter of her home. Apparently she does, because verse 5 says, "I arose to open to my beloved." But isn't that just like God?

From the dawn of creation, God loved us from the comfort of eternity, omnipotence, omniscience, and sinlessness. But when humanity's need for salvation knocked on the door of God's heart like the fist of the beloved upon the bed chamber, we found out that God's heart is awake to us. God, who for an eternity lived in freedom from the constraints of time, space, and limited knowledge, stepped from heaven to earth and put on a garment of flesh and mortality. Then God, who dwelled in the comfort of sinlessness and the beauty of holiness, decided to enter a world of imperfection and impiety and soil his feet in the degradation of humanity to become sin for our salvation to bring us out of the night, out of the cold, and into the shelter of his presence. Love can make one comfortable, but being in love will move one beyond his or her comfort zone.

That is why if we truly love God like we say we do, we can't keep doing the same old thing over and over again. Being in love means expanding our vision, experiencing new possibilities, expecting something new of ourselves and the God we love. Paul rightly said, "If anyone is in Christ, there is a new creation: everything old has passed away; see, everything has become new!" Being in love will move us from an old life to a new love. Being in love will move us from an old talk to a new walk. Being in love will move us from an old song to a new shout. Being in love will move us from old doubts to new faith. Being in love will move us from dead prayers to new power. Being in love will make one move, because one can love from a distance, but being in love means you cannot get close enough. Consider verses 5:6–8.

When the woman goes to receive her beloved, he has left. There is too much distance, too much space between them. She goes out to search for him, but he cannot be found. She calls, but he gives no answer. When the sentinels find her, they treat her like a prostitute. They beat her and take away her mantel, the sign of her decency. She has one last hope. If she cannot get to her beloved directly, she will send a message to him indirectly:

> I adjure you, O daughters of Jerusalem,
>   if you find my beloved,
> tell him this:
>   I am faint with love.
>
>   — 5:8

In other words, "Ain't no mountain high enough. Ain't no valley low enough. Ain't no river wide enough to keep me from gettin' to you."[5] But isn't that just like God?

In the Pentateuch, God spoke from heaven, but God still wasn't close enough. In the five books of the Law, God spoke through the Law, but God still wasn't close enough. Throughout the Old Testament, God spoke through prophets, priests, and kings — human intermediaries that stood between the people and God — but God still wasn't close enough. John 1:14 says, "the Word became flesh and lived among us," and God still wasn't close enough. In the ministry of Jesus, God searched for us like the woman in our text searched for her beloved, like the shepherd searched for one lost sheep, like the woman searched for one lost coin. God kept on searching even though some Roman sentinels stood in the way, beat him all night long, took away his garment, and hung him on a cross. And God still wasn't close enough.

That is why God now dwells in human hearts rather than in the Holy of Holies. That is why God dwells in all people who call upon the name of the Lord, not just the prophets, priests, and preachers. That is why God is Emmanuel — God with us. And God is God the Holy Spirit, God inside of us.

Yet God will never be close enough if we won't get close to God. If we have the presence of God in our lives and still won't pray, we are not yet close enough. If we have the Spirit of God inside of us but still won't seek God's face, we are not yet close enough. If we have the love of God inside of us, but still won't love each other, we are not yet close enough.

The deficiency is not in God's deeds or desires, because ain't no person mean enough, ain't no demon strong enough, ain't no sin bad enough to keep God away from us. And when God could not get to us directly, God sent a message to us indirectly. You tell them, Ezra, that the Lord's "steadfast love endures forever toward Israel" (Ezra 3:11). Tell them this, David, that "power belongs to God, and steadfast love belongs to [the LORD]" (Psalm 62:11–12). Prophesy, Isaiah, "You are precious in my sight, and honored, and I love you" (Isaiah 43:4). Tell them, Hosea, "I will heal their disloyalty; I will love them freely, for my anger has turned from them" (Hosea 14:4). Explain to them, John, that God "so loved the world, that he gave his only begotten Son, that whosoever believeth in him should not perish, but have eternal life" (John 3:16, KJV). Tell them, Paul, that "neither death, nor life, nor angels, nor rulers, nor things present, nor things to come, nor powers, nor height, nor depth, nor anything else in all creation, will be able to separate us from the love of God in Christ Jesus our Lord" (Romans 8:38–39). And with the eloquence of speech and the wisdom of the ages, write a song, Solomon, a *šîr hašîrîm*, a song of many songs, and tell them this: "I am faint with love" (Song of Solomon 5:8).

> Softly and tenderly Jesus is calling, calling for you and for me.
> See on the portals he's waiting and watching, watching for you and me.
> Come home, come home, ye who are weary come home
> Earnestly, tenderly Jesus is calling, calling, O sinner, come home.[6]

Notes

1. Elizabeth Barrett Browning, Sonnet 43 in *Sonnets from the Portuguese* (1850).
2. Lord Byron, "She Walks in Beauty," stanza 1 (1815).
3. Cain Hope Felder affirms the woman's African lineage by positing that she may be either the queen of Sheba or simply a Shulammite woman whose ancestor Gad is of African/Edenic origin. *The Original African Heritage Bible* (Iowa Falls, Iowa: World Bible Publishers, 1993), 991, 995. Jack S. Deere, in his introduction to the Song of Songs *(The Bible Knowledge Commentary)*, notes that some scholars identify the woman in the book as a daughter of Pharaoh; cf. 1 Kings 3:1. I have noted that

Gad and his son Shuni (ancestor of the Shulammites) sojourned in Egypt (Genesis 46:16), and their descendants were numbered among those in the wilderness (Numbers 26:18), suggesting that intermarriage with the Egyptians was very likely.

4. Ronald Murphy, "Song of Songs," in *Anchor Bible Dictionary*, ed. David Noel Freedman (New York: Doubleday, 1992), 6:151.

5. Nick Ashford and Valerie Simpson, "Ain't No Mountain High Enough."

6. Will L. Thompson, "Softly and Tenderly Jesus Is Calling."

11

The Gold of Ophir
Job 28:12–16

William D. Watley

When Job described wisdom in Job 28:12–16, he said that it superseded the value of the gold of Ophir. When I read this passage, I was struck by the words "gold of Ophir." I remembered that I had run across a number of references to the gold of Ophir at various times in my reading of the Old Testament. For example, in Job 22:24 there is another reference to the gold of Ophir. Psalm 45:9 refers to the queen being dressed in the gold of Ophir. In Isaiah 13:12 the prophet delivering an oracle for God declares, "I will make mortals more rare than fine gold, and humans than the gold of Ophir." In the apocryphal book Sirach we are told, "Do not exchange a friend for money or a real brother for the gold of Ophir" (7:18). In 1 Kings 9 and 10 we are told that Solomon imported 420 talents, or $12,337,290, of gold from Ophir. Also in 1 Kings 22:48 we read of the plans of Jehoshaphat to send a fleet of ships to Ophir for gold. In 1 Chronicles 29:4, David told his son Solomon that he was giving from his own personal treasury 3,000 talents, or $88,123,500, of gold from Ophir for the utensils and adornments for the house of the Lord.

The gold of Ophir was evidently the most highly prized gold in the ancient biblical world. Just as in today's world the Persian Gulf is known for its oil, Japan for its technology, Brazil for its gems, Paris for its perfumes, Evian for its mineral water, Napa Valley for its vineyards, and the United States for its military might, Ophir set the gold standard for the biblical world. But where is Ophir? Although various locations have been proposed, I accept the conclusion of the *Interpreter's Dictionary of the Bible* that Ophir is in East Africa in the vicinity of Somaliland.[1] In biblical times Ophir would probably have been either a part of or an extension of the Ethiopian kingdom, which ranged into southern Arabia. A round trip to Ophir from Ezion-geber, which was the main seaport of ancient Palestine, would take close to three years. The gold of Ophir was evidently so prized that the people from the biblical world were willing to take a journey of that length to get it.

The gold of Ophir is a reminder that a number of us need to rethink our image of Africa as a continent of only malaria infested jungles, sweltering heat, wild animals, and uncivilized natives. If such were the case, European nations would not have been in such a frenzy to get a piece of it and colonize it. Europeans fought each other for it and then fought indigenous people to keep control of it. Why? Because Africa is resource rich. Oil, gold, diamonds, copper, and exotic wildlife are still in abundance in Africa. No other continent has as great an abundance and variety of natural resources as Africa.

Africa is resource rich because God made it that way; he put those resources there at the creation. Humans can take no credit for Africa's resources. The finest and most prized gold in the Bible was in Ophir, in black Africa, because the hand of God planted it there. Let us never forget that we have natural resources planted within us by God. Some resources we acquire and develop through education and experience, but other resources have been placed within us by the hand of God. Others may close doors in our faces and set up stumbling blocks in our paths, but they cannot stop the flow of the natural resources that God has placed within us. Anyone who has ever overcome any human-made or devil-sent difficulty has made it because of the natural resources that keep on flowing no matter what others think or do.

We don't have to be jealous of anyone or resentful because someone else has advantages that we don't have. God has already given us all the natural resources we need to make it. We have a mind — let's use it. What do you do when you don't know what to do? *Think!* What do you do when after you have thought and you still don't know what to do? *Think some more.* If a solution is not readily evident, most of us consider a problem unsolvable. But no problem is unsolvable as long as we have a functioning brain. Think until your breakthrough comes. God gave us a brain so that we might be equipped to think through our difficulties. Let's use our brains for something besides worrying, pondering the petty, musing over messes, and gathering garbage over "what ifs."

We have a reasonable portion of health and strength. With a working mind and a functioning body, we are already resource rich. I visited a hospital and saw a friend who told me how he had visited the top floor and had seen accommodations for the wealthy. He said, "When you have money, they really know how to treat you well." I replied, "With all of their money, they are still sick. With all of their money, they are no better off than you are, because both you and they are in the hospital. And when you leave, some of them will still be here." What difference does a fancy room make when you are in a hospital? God gives health and strength. It is up to us to take care of what God has given us.

If we want something in life, God has given us natural resources to get it — a sound mind, a reasonable portion of health and strength, and opportunity. Every day is an opportunity. If you don't believe that a day is an opportunity, visit a morgue and ask those you see on slabs if they have any more opportunities to straighten out messes they made or to pursue any more dreams or goals. Many of us are quick to say, "I didn't have this or that — I didn't have a mother or father, a sponsor or mentor, or someone to help or guide me. I didn't have money or connections." But every year God sends 365 opportunities for us to find what we didn't have. If we are twelve years old, we have already had more than 4,380 opportunities. If we are twenty, we have already had more than 7,300 opportunities. If we are thirty, we have already had more than 10,950 opportunities. If we are forty, we have already had more than 14,600 opportunities. If we are fifty, we have already had more than 18,250 opportunities. If we are sixty, we have already had more than 21,900 opportunities. If we are seventy, we have already had more than 25,550 opportunities. If we are eighty, we have already had more than 29,200 opportunities. If we are ninety, we have already had more than 32,850 opportunities, and if we still have a sound mind and a reasonable portion of health and strength, what are we doing with opportunities that God keeps adding to our lives?

God has made us resource rich. We have sound minds, a reasonable portion of health and strength, opportunities, and prayer. While prayer is our most powerful natural resource, it only works in concert with the other resources. Prayer is not our sitting down and asking God to do for us what we can do for ourselves. A student once came to me and told me about all of the praying he was doing to prepare for one of my exams. After listening to him, I replied, "Fine, but have you studied?" Prayer is asking God to guide our thinking, strengthen our bodies, help us take full advantage of our opportunities, and then to do what we cannot do after we have done our best.

The first lesson from the gold of Ophir is a reminder about our natural resources. The gold of Ophir would forever remain where it is, however, unless someone mined it and refined it. That is the second lesson. Our natural resources will never be utilized to the fullest unless they are mined and refined by the right persons. The gold of Ophir was first mined and refined by the native Africans to whom it had been given. But when the European powers began to colonize the region, the gold mining and refining was taken over by them. The people to whom the resources belonged began to be oppressed, and what had been placed within their hands began to be exploited by others.

Are your natural resources being mined and refined, or are they being exploited? Are your mind, your body, your opportunities, your faith, and your love being mined and refined, or are they being exploited? Satan is not in the mining and refining business. He is an exploiter. Satan will take what God has given you and leave you with a confused mind, a spent body, wasted opportunities, and no prayer power. Selfish people will exploit what God has given you. They will pump your brain to help them push their agenda. They will use your body to gratify their lusts and their ego. You will waste your time and opportunities on those who are only out for self. And, if you are not careful, they will so drain you that you will start to blame God for what you allowed them to do. But thanks be to God, I know somebody who specializes in mining and refining the resources that God has placed within us. His name is Jesus. He told Peter and John, two fishermen, "Follow me, and I'll mine you and refine you. I'll make you fishers of persons." He told a Samaritan woman at the well who had been exploited by men, "If you allow me to mine you and refine you, I'll bring forth living water from you." After Jesus finished mining and refining the persecutor Saul, Saul became "Preacher Paul," who testified to the church at Rome based on his own personal experiences, "I appeal to you therefore, brothers and sisters, by the mercies of God, to present your bodies as a living sacrifice" (Romans 12:1). Jesus is still in the mining and refining business. He is still able to pull from us resources that God placed within us that even we didn't know were there.

The first lesson from the gold of Ophir is a reminder about our natural resources. The second lesson is a reminder that we need somebody to mine and refine us, and the third lesson from the gold of Ophir is that we need a craftsman. After the gold has been dug from the ground and mined and refined, it still has to be made into something. That is where the craftsman comes in. Whether the gold becomes a piece of fashion jewelry or a cross is in the hands of the craftsman. Spiritually speaking, God the Father plants the resource, God the Son mines and refines, and God the Holy Spirit is the craftsman. After Jesus saves us, the Holy Spirit begins to shape us into the final product. Some become preachers, some teachers, some workers, some have gifts of wisdom, music, faith, healing, discernment of spirits, various kinds of tongues, knowledge, administration, and helps.

When we think about what we have become, we must admit that God hasn't done badly with us or by us. We know that we are not perfect and that we have a long way to go to be like Jesus, but when we think about what the triune God has done with the lump of gold that others thought was brass and still others trash, we should be very grateful. God saw gold, and he mined, refined, and crafted us into a new creation. That should give us great joy.

Note

1. *Interpreter's Bible Dictionary*, Vol. 3 (Nashville: Abingdon Press, 1962), 605–606.

12

Raised with Rags and Ropes
Jeremiah 38:6–13

William D. Watley

Y ou can be on welfare, but you don't have to have a welfare mind — one that believes you are supposed to receive and spend rather than work and save. A welfare mind is one that is content to just get by from month to month without any dreams, determination, hope, or vision of doing better. And what is said of a people applies to an individual: Where there is no vision an individual perishes — and possibly his or her children.

You can be poor, but your mind doesn't have to be an impoverished mind. I am reminded of my grandmother. The only jobs I ever knew her to have were washing and ironing, and cleaning white people's houses. Every now and then she would have the opportunity of bringing me things that the children of the people for whom she worked would discard or had outgrown. Yet she never brought me their clothes and toys. Instead, she and my parents bought me the things they wanted me to have. My grandmother would, however, bring me their books. With a fifth grade education, she could barely read and write herself, yet she brought her grandson books. She was poor, but her mind was not.

You can be a janitor, a waitress, a salesclerk, or a servant and have what some people would refer to as a menial job as long as you remember that a janitor, a waitress, a clerk, a mail handler, or a servant is what you do to earn a living — it is not what you are. You are God's child of character and commitment, intelligence and integrity. You are a big person occupying a small spot. Because you know who and what you are, you don't allow your surroundings to determine your self-worth. You can be bigger than where you are and those around you.

Jeremiah 38:6–13 is a case in point. The prophet Jeremiah had been imprisoned because he had told the truth. He had learned the hard way that everyone who claims to want to hear the truth doesn't really want to hear it. More often than not people want to hear their own opinions and views agreed to by others. If you want to get into trouble with some people, if you want to lose friendship with some people, tell them the truth. Most of us go through life deciding between the truth and the politically wise thing to say, between the truth that angers and offends and the truth that is stretched or left unsaid, that consoles and doesn't create any waves.

Jeremiah was one of those persons who made people nervous because he was determined to tell the truth as he saw it. Tact was not his thing — truth was. Politics were not his thing — principles were. Ingenuity was not his thing — integrity was. Slyness was not his thing — sincerity was. Game playing was not his thing — genuineness was. You wouldn't want to ask Jeremiah his opinion of an outfit that was too tight or too gaudy. He would tell you. You wouldn't want to ask Jeremiah his opinion of your family or your children. He would tell you. You wouldn't want to ask Jeremiah his opinion of you, your lifestyle, or your values. He would tell you. And if you were the king, you wouldn't want to ask Jeremiah his opinion of your policies. He would tell you.

That was the mistake that Zedekiah, king of Judah, made when the Babylonians were preparing to attack Jerusalem. Zedekiah was preparing to hold out. But because Jeremiah believed the judgment of God was upon Judah, he advocated surrender. Some of the king's counselors and top officials, who had the most to lose, felt that Jeremiah should not be openly preaching a message of surrender and discouraging the hearts of the people and the morale of the soldiers. Thus, they imprisoned Jeremiah — they lowered him into a well with no water and left him there to die. And Jeremiah sank in the mud.

Picture Jeremiah, the devoted, uncompromising prophet of truth, sinking in the mud. Every life spends some time in the mud. Your faith hasn't really been tried until you have spent some time in the mud. Read the biographies of great men and women, and you will discover that before they made their great discovery, or wrote their literary masterpiece or musical score, or painted the picture that has carved them a place in immortality, they spent some time in the mud. Before they were inducted into the hall of fame or accomplished the great feats for which they are known or saw their dreams come true, they spent some time in the mud. They felt themselves sinking into the mud, where all seemed lost, where they felt forsaken and forlorn, where their lives seemed to be in vain and dreams seemed impossible to attain. Sometimes life and misfortune put us in the mud. Sometimes our miscalculations and mistakes, weaknesses, sins, and flaws put us in the mud. Sometimes other people, through meanness or envy, fear or resentment, put us in the mud. Sometimes Satan's attempts to break our faith and spirit put us in the mud.

Every marriage that survives has some mud on it. Every friendship or relationship of substance has some mud on it. Every dream that is realized has some mud on it. Every career, no matter how successful, has some mud on it. A faith strong and holy, noble and cleaned up, has some mud on it — mud that clings, stinks, and stains. Every life goes through the mud.

See Jeremiah in the mud asking God, "Why do the wicked prosper and scoundrels enjoy peace?" See Joseph lowered into the pit by jealous brothers — in the mud. See David playing crazy to save his life — in the mud. See Abraham lying instead of believing to protect himself — in the mud. See Noah, the most righteous of his generation, lying outside of his tent drunk and naked — in the mud. See Elijah running from Jezebel — in the mud. See Job cursing the day he was born — in the mud.

See John the Baptist locked up in prison and awaiting death wondering if Jesus is who John thought he was — in the mud. See Peter cursing and denying his Lord and then going off by himself and weeping bitterly — in the mud.

Have you ever been in the mud when it seems as if God has turned a deaf ear to your prayer, when living right and doing right doesn't seem to do any good after all? The harder you try the deeper you sink into the mud, where sin has you and you can't get out. When you find yourself in the mud, remember this truth: The mud is not your home. No matter how long we've been there, no matter how many times we've tried and failed to get out, the mud is not our home. That is the message that somebody needs to take to straying daughters, wayward sons, fallen wives, and backslidden husbands — the mud is not your home. Some of us have messed up careers, lost jobs and positions, broken hearts of those who loved us, disappointed those who believed in us — the mud is not your home. Some of us who are sick have been told by the devil that we aren't worth much and can't be productive. Don't believe it — the mud is not your home.

Whenever you find yourself in the mud for any reason, take a good long look at yourself in the mirror and say, "The devil is a liar — the mud is not my home. God can still make a way for me, Jesus' blood can still save me, the Holy Spirit can still work a miracle within me and upon me — the mud is not my home. I'm not dead yet. I still have a chance for recovery, for wholeness, for healing, for health — the mud is not my home. If God brought others out, God can bring me out — the mud is not my home. Even in the mud, God is good all the time. Therefore, the mud ought not be, will not be, cannot be, I'm not going to let it be — my home. Amen! Praise God! Thank you, Jesus! Hallelujah!

See Jeremiah feeling forsaken and forlorn, sinking in the mud. While he was sinking, however, help was coming from an unexpected source. In the king's household there was an Ethiopian eunuch, a son of Africa, a black man named Ebed-melech, who respected Jeremiah. He went to the king to plead Jeremiah's case.

When Jeremiah's own people had put this noble prophet in the mud, it was a black man who went to see about getting him out. Virtue defends and appreciates virtue. For Ebed-melech to defend Jeremiah, he had to be virtuous like the prophet. He had to have Jeremiah's integrity and honesty. He also had to have courage and convictions like Jeremiah.

A number of white racists and Eurocentric scholars have told us that blacks were uncivilized savages during biblical times. Evidently, they haven't read their Bibles and heard of the Queen of Sheba in Solomon's time, or Ebed-melech of Jeremiah's time, or Simon of Cyrene, who helped Jesus carry his cross. The uncivilized among Jeremiah's own people put him in the mud, but it was a humane, refined, articulate, intelligent, religious black man named Ebed-melech who understood that he was bigger than his surroundings, who tried to get the prophet out. He may not have had the riches of others, but he was not impoverished in his thinking and poor in his spirit. He knew he was God's child.

Ebed-melech told the king that those who put Jeremiah in the mud had acted wickedly against him. The king gave him permission to save Jeremiah. Ebed-melech didn't have any ladders to rescue Jeremiah, so he went to the storehouse and gathered rags and worn-out clothes, which he let down to Jeremiah in the cistern by ropes. He told the prophet to put the rags under his armpits between his body and the ropes. Then Ebed-melech lifted the prophet from the mud with rags and ropes.

Ebed-melech didn't have any sophisticated equipment; nor did he need any. He used what was available to him — rags and ropes. And although his equipment may not have been the best, his rags and ropes were sufficient to get the job done. Some of us know what it is to be saved by rags and ropes. When others took the ham and ate high off the hog, we took the rags and ropes — the feet, the ears, the tail, and the chitterlings, and fed ourselves until we could be better. I made it through school not only because of the scholarships I received, but because of the rags and ropes donations I was given. Some dear soul who never set foot on a college campus would put five or ten dollars in my hand and say, "I know it's not much, but maybe it will help get you a meal." Or some church would take up an offering and say, "Maybe this will help buy your books." Many days those rags and ropes donations put food on the table and gas in my car.

Black colleges and schools were built by rag and rope donations of people. Our churches are not endowed, but we survive and thrive because faithful, hard-working, Holy Spirit–guided people bring their little rag and rope offerings. When we bring them, they seem so small, but when we tie them all together, the Lord has a way of stretching them. Then we are able to let the salvation rope down into the mud, put the rags of hope under the frail arms of the sinking, and lift them out with love.

As a matter of fact, Christianity is a rag and rope religion. We are not saved by some great liturgical act or some marvelous intellectual theory, but by a carpenter's son who spent his life and ministry with people in the mud. The stinky fishermen and Galilean sod busters who were his disciples were muddy people. A much married woman at Jacob's well, a tax collector named Zacchaeus, lepers, prostitutes, a dying thief — those he ministered to and saved were all muddy people. One day on a hill called Calvary he bore a rag and rope rugged cross and died for my sins and your sins. He came to where we were in the mud and lifted us from grime to grace, sin to salvation, helplessness to hope, failure to faith, trouble to triumph, vice to victory, hell to heaven.

13

The African Woman Whom Jesus Praised
Matthew 12:42

William D. Watley

W hen I read Matthew 12:42, I am fascinated that Jesus praised an African woman. The African woman Jesus praised, however, was not living during Jesus' time on earth but had been dead for thousands of years. This means that she must have been so dynamic that she had become part of the religious and cultural tradition of the Hebrews to the extent that thousands of years after her life and death, Jesus heard, read, and learned enough about her to respect her and praise her.

Who was this African woman Jesus referred to as the "queen of the South"? She is the famous queen of Sheba, and her story appears in 1 Kings 10:1-13. Although Sheba is in southern Arabia, at the time this queen lived and ruled, Ethiopia was more of a region than the single nation we know today. It stretched beyond the borders of Africa to include southern Arabia. (Persons interested in further study of this great African queen are encouraged to read Cain Hope Felder's *Troubling Biblical Waters*.)[1]

According to 1 Kings 10:1-13, the queen of Sheba lived at a time when King Solomon was at the height of his reign and Israel was regarded as a world power. Even during his lifetime the wisdom of Solomon and the greatness of his kingdom were approaching legendary proportions to the extent that the curiosity of the queen of Sheba, as a major world power herself, was piqued. To see for herself what she had heard about, she left her home and traveled to the capital of the Solomonic kingdom with a great retinue. Travel in that era was not what it is today in terms of either convenience or quickness. The queen had to travel at least fifteen hundred miles to visit Solomon, and considering the size of her caravan, her journey easily could have taken several months one way. No wonder Jesus said she had come from the ends of the earth.

First of all, the queen had to have been extremely secure as a ruler to leave her kingdom for such a long a period of time. I do not know of one world ruler today of her stature who could be absent from office for half a year or more and still have his or her power intact. Second, since Solomon's wisdom was legendary, she had to be secure in her own abilities and intelligence to approach him as an equal. Scripture tells us that she didn't simply come to sit at his feet as a disciple, but she came as his equal. She came to test him with hard questions. Third, if Solomon was supposed to be the best, the queen's long and costly journey to meet Solomon meant that she had a desire for the best.

Some of us are comfortable only with mediocrity or someone to whom we feel superior. Look at a person's friends, and you can tell a lot about how secure a person is. Insecure people only get close to people to whom they feel superior in terms of looks, age, education, position, or financial status. Insecure people feel that they must have some kind of edge on others so that others will look up to them as a superior rather than looking at them as an equal eyeball to eyeball. Some people will not get close to you unless they can advise you, boss you, or run your business. Some people will dislike you and will feel threatened by you if in their shallow opinion you look as good as they do, know as much as they do, or speak, sing, cook, or dress as well as they can.

I once went to a tailor who, before he did anything, stood back and looked at me from head to toe. He walked around me and studied me. Before he even took a tape measure to me, he had just about sized me up. For some people every relationship is political, a contest of one-upmanship. Some people start sizing people up the minute they meet them. If such people conclude that you are enough of an equal to threaten them by whatever power, position, or prestige they think you have, they will develop an almost immediate disdain for you and start working against you behind your back.

The queen of Sheba was not like this. She was secure enough in who she was to search out the best. She understood that it takes the best to bring out the best in us. People who know only as much as we do cannot add to our knowledge. People who have been exposed only to what we have been exposed to cannot add to our experience. If we are in a pit or a hole, whether it is a sin hole, an ignorance hole, a depression hole, or a money hole, we need someone stronger to pull us out. Intelligence breeds intelligence, class breeds class, and spirituality breeds spirituality. If we want to grow, we have to be around somebody who can help us grow.

The queen of Sheba wanted the best for herself, so she traveled from the ends of the earth to the best in her time. Secure people not only search for the best, they don't mind admitting that they have needs. Some people are in dire straits today and are about to lose their jobs, homes, minds, families, and health because they are too insecure to ask for help. They claim they don't want other people to know their business. Well, if your life falls apart, people are going to know your business anyway. Sometimes people won't share their pain, and then they get an attitude if other people don't offer to help them. People are not mind readers. How are they supposed to know what we are feeling unless we tell them? If we have needs, we ought to have enough security and self-confidence, like the queen of Sheba, to search out the best resources. She didn't go to just any king. She sought the best king who had the ability to help her. Likewise, we shouldn't tell our business to just anybody. We share our needs with those who are big enough to help. Only the ignorant and the insecure try to be what they are not, pretend to know what they do not, and claim to have what they do not. Only the ignorant and insecure say that they are doing just fine when the bottom of life is about to fall out. If you are drowning, you had better quit pretending that you are fine and then open your mouth and yell for help.

The queen of Sheba had needs, so she came to the best and questioned Solomon. She didn't pretend that she knew everything — she questioned. She didn't say, "What will other people think if I lay my concerns before Solomon?" She questioned. She didn't accept everything she was told without using the mind God had given her to think things through — she questioned. Secure people not only search for the best and admit their needs, they also don't mind sharing their blessings and helping others. Solomon was also secure. Thus, as the queen of Sheba asked, he answered; and as she sought, he shared.

First Kings 10:3 tells us that "Solomon answered all her questions; there was nothing hidden from the king that he could not explain to her." Not only did he answer her questions, but he also showed her how much God had blessed him. The tour of his administration not only included the royal stables, the palace he had built, the food on his table, and the attendance of his servants, but he also took the queen to the house of the Lord. There she saw his devotion and sacrifices. A truly wise and secure person knows how to give God glory.

When the queen of Sheba had seen and heard sufficiently, she said, "The report was true that I heard in my own land of your accomplishments and of your wisdom, but I did not believe the reports until I came and my own eyes had seen it" (1 Kings 10:6–7). Some things we have to see with our own eyes and know from our own experience. That is why the psalmist declared, "O taste and see that the LORD is good" (Psalm 34:8). That's why Job could say, "I had heard of you by the hearing of the ear, but now my eye sees you" (Job 42:5). Consequently, when people don't believe your witness, don't argue with them, just say to them like Philip to Nathanael, "Come and see" (John 1:46). And if you really want to know what God can and will do for you, "Come and see."

The queen of Sheba continued, "Not even half had been told me; your wisdom and prosperity far surpass the report that I had heard" (1 Kings 10:7). Secure people don't mind giving others credit. Only insecure people try to lessen or make light of the achievements or blessings of others, failing to give credit to others for their accomplishments. People are smart and know what they know whether we give them proper recognition or not. People are good looking whether we like them or not. If people are talented, they can still do what they can do whether we appreciate it or not. Failing to recognize people for who and what they are doesn't take anything away from them. It only shows how small and petty we are. Great people do not need our recognition to be great. Great people will be great no matter where they are — in the kitchen or on a throne. David was as great in the fields as a shepherd as he was on the throne as a king. Jesus was as great when he was dealing with children and sinners as he was when he was stilling storms. His greatness was simply reflected in different ways. He was great on Mount Calvary; he was great on the Mount of Transfiguration; he was great when restoring Peter; and he was great when feeding the five thousand. Only small people need others to make them important or great.

The queen of Sheba gave Solomon a thank offering. First Kings 10:10–12 says:

> Then she gave the king one hundred twenty talents of gold, a great quantity of spices, and precious stones; never again did spices come in such quantity as that which the queen of Sheba gave to King Solomon.
> Moreover, the fleet of Hiram, which carried gold from Ophir, brought from Ophir a great quantity of almug wood and precious stones. From the almug wood the king made supports for the house of the Lord, and for the king's house, lyres also and harps for the singers; no such almug wood has come or been seen to this day.

In return Solomon gave the queen a "blessing gift." First Kings 10:13 says, "Meanwhile King Solomon gave to the queen of Sheba every desire that she expressed, as well as what he gave her out of Solomon's royal bounty. Then she returned to her own land, with her servants." Note that Solomon and the queen were not giving tokens of appreciation to each other, "but gifts from the heart." A token comes from the pocket, but a gift comes from the heart. If you give somebody something, don't ever call that a token if it is from your heart no matter how small it is.

Note the generosity of Solomon and the queen of Sheba. I have never known a person to be really secure and really great yet cheap and stingy at the same time. When we are insecure, we hold our fist tight, but when we are secure, we open our hands, because that is how we receive more. If we are secure in our relationship with God, we can easily afford to be generous, because we understand that we can't out-give God. Solomon and the queen of Sheba gave of their best to each other. Secure people give of their best because they have received the best and they know the best giver.

When Jesus observed how the queen of Sheba sought the best, brought the best she had and gave it, and received the best from the best of her day, who was Solomon, he had to praise her. He told the people of his day that she would rise up at the judgement and condemn them because she came from the ends of the earth to listen to the wisdom of Solomon, and someone greater than Solomon was now present. What Jesus said about his generation applies to us as well. My word of warning is this: Don't let the queen of Sheba condemn you, because we have a King greater than Solomon. Solomon was wise, but our King is the Way, the Truth, and the Life. Solomon could bestow riches; our King grants righteousness, plus, plus, plus....Solomon gave the queen of Sheba the desires of her heart; our King will bless us not only with the desires of our heart, but also with deliverance from bondage. Solomon knew some things; our King knows all things. Solomon had some power; our King has all power. Solomon reigned for a while, our King reigns forever. In his old age, Solomon's heart turned away from God, but hear our King's last words from the cross: "Father, into your hands...." When Solomon died, his kingdom split, but the kingdom of Jesus Christ keeps right on growing. When Solomon died he stayed dead, but when our King died, he rose again to live forevermore. Solomon was a king, but Jesus Christ is the King of Kings.

The queen of Sheba had to travel a long distance and a long time to reach Solomon, but right now, if we call on the name of Jesus right where we are, we can make contact with him. He will hear, and he will answer.

Note

1. Cain Hope Felder, *Troubling Biblical Waters* (Maryknoll, N.Y.: Orbis Books, 1989), 22–36.

14

More Than a Momentary Experience

Mark 15:21; Romans 16:13

William D. Watley

T he name of Simon of Cyrene — the North African who, according to the Synoptic Gospels, bore the cross for Jesus when our Lord, weary from his night-long ordeal of being tried and mocked, repeatedly fell on his way to Calvary — does not appear elsewhere in the gospel accounts. One could almost conclude that after the cross-bearing experience, Simon of Cyrene simply dropped out of the life of the Christian church. The small reference in Mark's gospel and a greeting in Paul's letter to the Romans, however, indicate that such was not the case. Simon of Cyrene evidently had more than a momentary experience of cross-bearing for Jesus.

Mark introduced Simon of Cyrene by saying, "They compelled a passer-by, who was coming in from the country, to carry his cross; it was Simon of Cyrene, the father of Alexander and Rufus" (15:21). The names of Alexander and Rufus would be known by members of the early church only if they were active in the life of the church. Mark, the earliest of the Gospels, was written thirty to forty years after Jesus' death and resurrection. Evidently, the sons of the North African Simon of Cyrene were so active that Mark could mention their names assuming that the community of faith would recognize them.

If Alexander and Rufus were active, where were they active?

Paul answers that question in Romans 16 when he sends personal greetings to members of the church of Rome. In verse 13 he writes, "Greet Rufus, chosen in the Lord; and greet his mother — a mother to me also." Note what Paul calls Rufus — "chosen in the Lord." Paul didn't just throw compliments around. Rufus had to have been a very special believer to receive that kind of compliment from Paul. Note what he calls Rufus's mother, the wife of the North African Simon of Cyrene, "a mother to me also." The church at Rome was a major congregation in the life of the early church. Its very location made it pivotal. And, apparently, one of the leading families in this key congregation was a North African family whose father thirty years before had helped Jesus carry his cross. When Simon of Cyrene reached Calvary, he must not have walked away. He must have become such a believer that thirty years later his sons and widow had become ardent believers and famous Christians themselves.

I don't know at what point Simon of Cyrene began to take an active interest and close look at Jesus. Perhaps a curiosity was sparked while he was bearing the cross. Perhaps he noticed Jesus' peacefulness on his way to Calvary. He was not acting like the average criminal whose crime had been so serious that death by crucifixion was the sentence. He did not curse or spit back at the crowd or at the Roman soldiers. Jesus was calm as if he knew something others didn't know. He was acting as if he could look beyond present circumstances and see his victory. True, it hadn't arrived yet. The crown of thorns was still on his head, fierce enemies and fearful followers were still around him, agony was still awaiting him, and death was preparing to claim him. But Jesus knew that no matter what happened to him, when it was all over, he would have the victory. So in the midst of stress and strain, he showed tremendous strength of character.

That is what faith is all about — knowing for certain that things will turn out as they have been revealed even when everything appears to be going wrong. You might not know when, or where, or how, but you know that victory is coming. It is just up the road a ways, just around the bend. It is just a few more risings and settings of the sun. If not today, then tomorrow; if not tomorrow, then next week; if not next week, then next month; if not this year, then next year — but it will come. Victory has to come, because God is still in the blessing business, the miracle-working and way-making business. It has to come because God is true to God's word — "All things work together for good for those who love God, who are called according to his purpose" (Romans 8:28). It has to come, because God has not brought us this far to leave us. It has to come, because Calvary didn't have the last word; God did.

So if, like Jesus, you are still on this side of Calvary, if the devil is whispering in your ear, "I got you now," and everything seems to indicate that the devil is right, remember whose you are and stay calm. Even in trouble God is still closer than your breath and nearer than your hands and feet. Besides, there is a Simon of Cyrene following behind observing how you work through your problems, and if you remain faithful, keeping your victory in view, when it comes, your example will have helped to save a Simon.

I don't know the moment Simon of Cyrene became a believer. Perhaps his observation of how Jesus carried himself as Simon walked behind him to Calvary had an impact. And if when he reached Calvary he stayed around a while, I'm sure that he would have been deeply moved, because he would have heard Jesus pray for his enemies, "Father, forgive them; for they do not know what they are doing" (Luke 23:34). He would have seen him tell a dying thief, "Today you will be with me in Paradise" (Luke 23:43). He would have observed Jesus caring for his mother, "Woman, here is your son" (John 19:26). He would have seen the Lord's utter loneliness when he cried out, "My God, my God, why have you forsaken me?" (Mark 15:34). He would have observed the Lord's humanity when he said, "I am thirsty" (John 19:28). He would have learned how to pray through when Jesus declared, "It is finished" (John 19:30). And he would have heard Jesus' shout of triumph when he said, "Father, into your hands I commend my spirit" (Luke 23:46).

If Simon had remained at the cross, he would have beheld a midnight darkness cover the land from noon until three o'clock in the afternoon, the hottest and brightest part of the day. He would have felt the earth reel and rock like a drunken man. He would have seen a hardened Roman centurion on crucifixion duty be moved to confess, "Truly this man was God's Son!" (Mark 15:39). If Simon had stayed around, he couldn't have helped but be moved by all that he saw and heard.

I don't know about you, but Calvary always moves me. When I think about all that Jesus went through for me, I'm always moved. When I think of the goodness of Jesus and all he's done for me, my soul cries out, "Hallelujah! Thank God for saving me!" One school of preaching says that a preacher should never close a sermon without touching Calvary. The older I get, the more I understand why. Perhaps Moses' parting of the Red Sea doesn't do anything, or the three Hebrew boys seem like a fantasy, and Daniel in the lion's den seems like fiction, but the story of God's love is able to reach the hardest of hearts.

I don't know when Simon became a believer. Perhaps it started when he began to carry the cross and then continued at Calvary. And after the Lord's resurrection and before his ascension, perhaps Simon was one of those who beheld Jesus in one of his postresurrection appearances. If so, he would have seen firsthand what God can still do for you when the devil has done everything to break you. And even though you have the marks of Calvary upon you, you still have resurrection glory, answered prayer glory, victory anyhow glory. When you have helped someone carry a cross, when you have watched that person suffer, when you know for a fact that that person should be over and done with, and yet he or she stands before you with a testimony that says, "Look where Jesus brought me from" and "See what the Lord has done," that's enough to make you a believer.

Who knows? Perhaps Simon was in the upper room or in the crowd that gathered on the outside on the day of Pentecost. Perhaps he heard Peter say:

This is what was spoken through the prophet Joel:

"In the last days it will be, God declares,
that I will pour out my Spirit upon all flesh,
    and your sons and your daughters shall prophesy,
and your young men shall see visions,
    and your old men shall dream dreams."

— Acts 2:16–17

Perhaps Simon heard the question, "Brothers, what should we do?" (Acts 2:37). If he had, he would have heard the answer, "Repent, and be baptized every one of you in the name of Jesus Christ so that your sins may be forgiven; and you will receive the gift of the Holy Spirit. For the promise is for you, for your children, and for all who are far away, everyone whom the Lord our God calls to him" (Acts 2:38–39).

I don't know when Simon became a believer, but I do know that his time with Jesus and his experience of Jesus had to be more than a momentary encounter of cross-bearing to Calvary. He had to have had some other experiences that didn't make it into the record. Sometimes it's the off-the-record experiences that tell the real story. You remember those times when we were by ourselves and nobody was around to see it or record it, but we felt the presence of the Most High God. We had a personal visit with Jesus. We felt the anointing of the Holy Spirit. Our breakthrough came. We got a feeling that everything was going to be all right.

We don't know when, how, or where Simon became a believer. Something had to have happened to change him from a reluctant passerby who was compelled to carry a cross into Simon, father of Alexander, well-known church leader, and father of Rufus, chosen of the Lord, and husband of the woman whom the apostle Paul said was like a mother to him.

Simon didn't stop with the cross-bearing experience. He must have gone all the way with Jesus. No matter where you are in the Lord, no matter what the Lord has already done, don't stop now. There's more in store — more promises to be kept, more power to be received, more battles to be fought, more victories to be won. There's a deeper and higher place to be reached, but we have to go all the way with Jesus.

A rich young ruler had a great moment with Jesus, but he didn't go all the way and walked away heavyhearted. Pilate had a great conversation with Jesus, but he didn't go all the way and ended up turning Jesus over to a bloodthirsty mob. Judas had great times with Jesus, but he didn't go all the way and ended up betraying the Lord. John went all the way and could testify, "Beloved, we are God's children now . . . " (1 John 3:2). Paul went all the way and could say, "I have fought the good fight . . . " (2 Timothy 4:7). Peter went all the way and could testify, "You know that you were ransomed from the futile ways inherited from your ancestors, not with perishable things like silver or gold, but with the precious blood of Christ" (1 Peter 1:18–19). Martin Luther King Jr. went all the way and could say, "I've been to the mountaintop. . . . "

Religion is about more than a good feeling or emotion that lasts only for a moment. It is about going all the way. Down in Georgia I used to hear people sing, "Let Jesus lead you, let Jesus lead you, let Jesus lead you all the way. All the way from earth to heaven, let Jesus lead you all the way." Or as somebody said, "Where he leads me I will follow, I'll go with him all the way."

15

Seized, Saved, and Set Apart
Luke 23:26

William D. Watley

He was just a passerby standing on the sidelines in the crowd. When he arrived in Jerusalem from the rural areas during the Passover season, like a number of others, he had no idea that Jesus was being crucified. Cyrene, from which he came, is located in North Africa and today would be found in the country of Libya. His name, Simon, indicates the influence of Jewish culture upon his life, and his presence in Jerusalem indicates an interest in the Lord God Almighty.

Thus, Simon, a black African from Cyrene in North Africa, was casually walking through one of the crowded streets of Jerusalem during the Passover season when he noticed some kind of disturbance or procession ahead. A small group of Roman soldiers was clearing a path through the streets. Standing on tiptoe and straining his neck, Simon could see several men struggling to carry crosses. As the procession drew closer, Simon stepped to the side to get out of the way. He could see beneath the helmets of the Roman soldiers sweat running down their faces. He could hear their curses as they roughly pushed people out of their way. Occasionally he had to shield his eyes as the spears and shields of the soldiers caught the late morning sunlight and flashed in his eyes.

He could hear the sharp snap of a whip as it came down on

the backs of the men carrying the crosses. He could hear their muffled groans. He could hear the crowd's jeers and cries of "Crucify him! Crucify him!" Occasionally someone would spit on them and someone else would throw a piece of garbage at them. Simon happened to notice that some of those doing the jeering, spitting, and throwing were well-dressed, finely robed, long-bearded Pharisees and Sadducees wearing phylacteries and prayer shawls.

How strange, Simon thought to himself, *to see these distinguished religious leaders acting in such an uncouth way. I wonder who these men are? They really must have done something terrible to arouse such bitterness from such godly men.* Yet as Simon looked through the crowd, he could also see ordinary women and men standing in silence with tears running down their cheeks. Some fell on their knees in prayer. Some shook their heads in disbelief and wrung their hands in anguish.

The press and surge of the crowd was almost unbearable. Simon thought to himself, *I'll be glad when this procession passes so that I can continue to the bazaar.* Suddenly Simon was jarred back to the scene unfolding before him. One of the men carrying a cross had stumbled and fallen right in front of him — right at his feet. "Captain!" one of the soldiers called. "He's fallen again!" Simon saw a big, burly captain turn around and walk impatiently back to where the victim had fallen. "What? Again?" he said impatiently. He snapped at the soldiers, "What do you expect? You kept him up all night long beating him and mocking him."

Simon looked down at the wooly head and olive skin of the fallen cross-bearer and saw him struggling to breathe. Then Simon looked up and inadvertently caught the eye of the captain, who was looking at the crowd. According to Roman law, a soldier had the right to seize anybody out of the crowd to carry a prisoner's cross. Simon quickly looked away, but out of the corner of his eye he could see the big, rough Roman captain coming toward him. Simon tried to step back into the crowd, but they were pushing against him. He could feel his heart pounding as he kept looking down and praying to himself, "Please let him be coming for someone else."

Then Simon felt a yank on his shoulder and found himself in the middle of the procession with the captain pointing to the fallen man's cross and barking, "Pick it up."

"What?" Simon asked.

"I said, 'Pick it up,'" the Roman captain ordered. "But...," Simon said. The captain raised his whip, and the other Roman soldiers reached for their swords. Simon extended his black muscled North African arm to the fallen man to lift him up. As he did so, the fallen man lifted his head, and for the first time their eyes met. Simon was taken aback by what he saw. He expected to see the hardened, hate-filled eyes of an embittered criminal. But in this man's eyes he saw pain and power, love and loneliness, toughness and tenderness, compassion and courage, kindness and kingliness, suffering and steadfastness, heartbrokenness and heaven-boundness. It seemed as if this man, whoever he was, was carrying the weight of the world's sins upon his shoulders.

They might have stared at each other longer, but their moment was broken by the shout of the captain barking, "Come on, we ain't got all day." They nodded to each other, and Jesus, the prophet from Galilee, straightened himself and walked behind the Roman captain while Simon shouldered the burden of the cross that would one day become the symbol of humanity's redemption.

As Simon wrapped his muscular, ebony biceps around the cross and looked around at the mixed crowd expressing hatred and horror, curses and cries, he couldn't help but ask himself, "What am I doing, and how did I get here? How did I get mixed up in all of this mess?" Have you ever had to ask yourself that question when you found yourself in places where you should not have been and doing what you know you shouldn't have been doing? "What am I doing here? How did I get here? How did I get mixed up in all of this mess?" That's what the prodigal son must have asked himself when he came to himself in a hog pen. That's what the woman caught in adultery and brought before Jesus to be stoned must have asked herself. That's what Judas, when he realized his mistake in betraying Jesus, must have asked himself. That's what Simon Peter must have said to himself when he found himself cursing and denying that he knew the Lord.

Someone who has made a mistake and that mistake has caught up with him or her is asking those questions. Someone who has found a relationship on the rocks is asking those questions. Someone whose private business is in the streets and is facing public embarrassment and humiliation is asking those questions. Someone who can't seem to say no when he or she wants to say yes, or who can't break a habit that has him or her bound is asking those questions. Someone whose career is in trouble is asking those questions.

Simon was in the position he was in because he was seized unexpectedly by Roman soldiers. Likewise, sometimes we can be seized by the unexpected. We are just passing by when we become seized by temptations, seized by wrong thoughts, seized by Satan, seized by sin. We are in the wrong place at the wrong time, and all of a sudden we find ourselves caught in the middle of someone else's problems. My family has been seized by controversy, by accidents, by the unanticipated, by the uncalculated, and by the unheard of. Have you ever been seized by the unexpected?

Scripture says that when the soldiers seized Simon, they put him behind Jesus. They put him close to the Savior. I imagine that as Simon began to struggle with the cross — if we don't have to struggle with it, then it isn't a cross — sweat began to fall into his eyes, clouding his vision. Simon may have said to himself, "I can't see clearly, so I'll just stay focused on the footsteps of the one in front of me. Wherever he walks, I will walk."

Yes, all of us can be seized by the unexpected, but remember that when that happens, the Savior is near. Even though Jesus was on his way to Calvary, he had not lost any of his power. He could have called ten thousand angels to destroy the world and set him free. He was on his way to Calvary, not because he was sentenced, but because he was a Savior. He lived as Savior, he died as Savior, and he arose as Savior. Even in his weakest and worst moments, Jesus was still Savior.

Even in the worst of circumstances, Jesus is still Savior. Therefore, if you have been seized, remember that the Savior is only a prayer away, a plea away, a cry away, a groan away, a whisper away, a thought away. If, like Peter, you find yourself seized by fear while you are out in the midst of the storm, all you have to know is a three-word prayer — "Lord, save me" — and he will save you. Like Simon, stay focused on Jesus. For that to happen, Jesus has to be in front of you. Some of us try to run ahead of the Lord when we're seized. But if we stay focused on Jesus, his footsteps will lead us from Calvary to conquering. His Word will always be fulfilled, for his faithfulness outlasts our fickleness.

Simon is not heard of before this cross-bearing incident. Nor is he mentioned again in the Gospels. Out of all of the people we meet in the Gospels, Simon, the black man from North Africa, is set apart as the man who helped Jesus bear the cross. When we're seized, not only are we saved, but we are also set apart for the Redeemer's purposes, for God's glory, for the Holy Spirit's anointing. That is why none of us has to be jealous of anyone else's talent. That is why none of us has to try to be like anyone else. When we are saved after we have been seized, the Holy Spirit will give us our own testimony, bless us with our own gifts, fill us with our own fire, find work for our hands to do, and find paths of service for our feet to walk. He will set each of us apart and give us our own light to shine.

Did Simon preach three thousand souls into the kingdom like Peter? No! Did he establish churches like Paul? No! Did he provide a place for the Lord's body like Joseph of Arimathea? No! Simon of Cyrene is set apart because he bore a cross for Jesus. What are our lives set apart for? Is there another Simon in the house? "Must Jesus bear the cross alone and all the world go free?"

16

Who Is My Neighbor?
Luke 10:25–29

Raquel Annette St. Clair

"In 1492 Columbus sailed the ocean blue" the rhyme goes. And for more years than I care to remember, the "new world" has honored a man whose invasion into the Americas resulted in the abuse of Native American women, the slaughtering of the indigenous people, and the theft of their lands and material possessions.

Over four hundred years ago the slave trade began. Hundreds of millions of Africans were stolen from their homes, families, and loved ones. Untold millions died in the Middle Passage. Those who did survive were stripped of everything they possessed, even the ownership of their very bodies.

Before World War II was over, six million Jews were dead. Their homes and businesses were confiscated. They were packed together like animals and taken to concentration camps — men, women, and children.

And as we scan the pages of history, even the pages of today's newspapers, we often are horrified by the way humanity mistreats humanity. We see children killing children to prove their manhood or womanhood, or just to get a pair of sneakers. We see hate crimes and violent beatings because the victim does not look like or talk like the attacker. We see husbands beating wives, parents abusing children, and the young neglecting the elderly.

We live in a society dominated by "I," "me," and "my"

mentalities. We have forgotten one of Martin Luther King Jr's moral axioms: "We are all tied in a single garment of destiny, woven with an inescapable thread of mutuality. I can never be everything that I ought to be until you are everything that you ought to be. Therefore, ask not for whom the bell tolls, it tolls for thee."[1] In all of the above examples of mistreatment, I believe that one question is being asked: Who is my neighbor? It may not be said in those exact words, but somewhere in the dark recesses of one's heart, somewhere in the crowded corners of one's mind, "Who is my neighbor?" is asked and answered and the answer is acted upon.

The conquistadores and Christopher Columbus decided that Native Americans were not their neighbors. So they stole what they wanted and converted with the sword rather than with the Word of God. Slave traders and slave owners decided that Europeans and Euro-Americans were their neighbors. Thus, it was acceptable to enslave, sell, and breed Africans but not Europeans. Nazis had a very select group of neighbors — so select that few could meet their criteria.

Yet the history of asking this question goes further back than the Holocaust, further back than the slave trade, further back than the conquistadores, even further back than this New Testament passage. For if we look at the formation of ancient Israel recorded in the Old Testament, the same question was asked and answered, and the answer was acted upon.

In Exodus we have the Ten Commandments, or Decalogue, words believed to have been spoken from the mouth of God. On the surface they seem all-inclusive and universally binding. But in practice, only the rights of Israelites were protected under these laws. The Israelites were not responsible for treating "others" as neighbors. Stealing in the Old Testament is only called stealing when something is taken from the God of Israel or from an Israelite, not when the Israelites take land, lives, or possessions from others. So, yes, both our sacred and secular history attest to the asking of this question.

Lest we get too comfortable in our modern-day distance from those asking this question, lest we think this is someone else's problem, we must understand that this question isn't limited to the past. We ask it today, only in different ways. In the office, we replace "neighbor" with "colleague." In the church, we replace "neighbor" with "sister" or "brother." In general, we replace "neighbor" with "friends" or "buddies."

We ask this question every time we make a decision about whom to include and whom to exclude, because we cannot look past someone's eye color, skin color, hair texture, dress, or speech. We do it every time we cannot look past someone's bank account or lack thereof, or someone's religion, denomination, or gender. We do it every time we cannot look beyond someone's past mistakes, mess-ups, and problems.

We ask, "Who is my neighbor?" and give the answer when we can't look past all these things and see another human being created in the image of God and loved by God just as we are, with all of our imperfections, faults, and funny ways. We ask it and answer it every time we forget Dr. King's words that "human worth lies in relatedness to God."[2]

Humanity often asks God this question, and like the lawyer in Luke 10:25–29, we too want to be justified — in our hatred, biases, and exclusions and in the hypocrisy of allowing exclusions, divisions, and schisms — and still serve a God who says, "Whosoever will, let them come."

If the truth be told, we have already answered the question; we just want divine validation. "Who is my neighbor, dear Jesus?" Please let it be the people I already like. Then I can continue doing what I've always done. I can continue treating people like I've been treating them and mistreating people like I've been mistreating them or simply continue ignoring them. I can keep the schisms and the "isms" that define my life, and I don't have to change, repent, or move from my comfort zone.

Instead, Jesus tells us this story:

> "A man was going down from Jerusalem to Jericho, and fell into the hands of robbers, who stripped him, beat him, and went away, leaving him half dead. Now by chance a priest was going down that road; and when he saw him, he passed by on the other side. So likewise a Levite, when he came to the place and

saw him, passed by on the other side. But a Samaritan while traveling came near him; and when he saw him, he was moved with pity. He went to him and bandaged his wounds, having poured oil and wine on them. Then he put him on his own animal, brought him to an inn, and took care of him. He next day he took out two denarii, gave them to the innkeeper, and said, 'Take care of him; and when I come back, I will repay you whatever more you spend.' Which of these three, do you think, was a neighbor to the man who fell into the hands of the robbers?" He said, "The one who showed him mercy." Jesus said to him, "Go and do likewise." (Luke 10:30–37)

We still have not received our answer to the question. We asked, "Who is my neighbor?" and Jesus answered, "Go and do likewise." Go and do likewise. Jesus, why didn't you answer our question? Probably because we have been asking the wrong question all along. When we define who our neighbor is, we also define who are neighbor is not.

Let my neighbor be Sally. She dresses like me. Let my neighbor be Bob. He talks like me. Let my neighbor be Frank. He thinks like me. But what about Susie, who shops at the discount shop instead of at the mall like you? What about Mike, who learned English as a second language? What about Sam, who does not see the world the way you do?

If these were not on my original list of neighbors, I could mistakenly think that they are not my neighbors at all. Every time we ask, "Who is my neighbor?" we put the burden of proof on someone else. If we share the same racial/ethnic or religious background; if we occupy the same social class; if I like the way you look, act, think, or dress; if you have something I want, I need, I don't have, or cannot get; then we can be neighbors, friends, pals, and buddies. We end up limiting Christian love to reciprocal relationships.

But I heard Jesus say that sinners love those who love them. Sinners lend money to those who can pay them back. Sinners do good to those who are good to them. What makes the people of God any different than the people of the world? What makes the saint different than the sinner?

It only stands to reason that the wrong question yields the wrong answer, and the wrong answer yields the wrong action. In this story, Jesus gives us a new course of action. He issues a challenge to act, to do, and to be. He says, "Go and do likewise." In other words, "Be a neighbor."

We cannot sit around waiting for someone to be our neighbor or to prove that he or she can be a neighbor. Each one of us is called to take the initiative. We must treat people like we want to be treated first. We must love people the way we want to be loved first. We must accept people the way we want to be accepted first. We must understand the way we want to be understood first.

Nowhere in Jesus' story are there instructions for looking for a neighbor. Jesus does, however, give a few guidelines about how to be a neighbor. When we consider the way the New Testament writers depict the relationship (or, rather, lack of relationship) between Jews and Samaritans, we might have expected the Samaritan to cross over to the other side too. Even though the Jews and Samaritans were geographic and cultural neighbors — the Samaritans occupying the northern portion of Palestine, where the two half African tribes of Ephraim and Manasseh settled, the Jews' opinion of them was far from neighborly. Even the title of this pericope in many translations of the Bible as "The Good Samaritan" shows that we too share the Jews' bias. To call the protagonist of the story "the Good Samaritan" implies that the rest of the Samaritans were not good people and that this man was an exception to the rule. It is the modern-day equivalent of calling "respectable" and "acceptable" African Americans "good negroes."[3]

The first lesson the Samaritan teaches us is to let go of the preconceptions that divide us from one another. The Samaritan treated the wounded man like a neighbor regardless — regardless of his age, race, gender, or religion. He did not ask if he was AME, CME, UMC, ABC, NBC, PBC, PCA, or PCUSA. He saw a man in need and worked to fill that need. He shows us that ministry does not always take place among the people we prefer, in the places we expect, or under the conditions we want.

Ministry is not always safe, sanitary, or secure. But the Samaritan let all of his preferences and preconceptions go to demonstrate love to a person who may never have been in a position to do the same for him. And that is what we are called to do. If we are ever going to be a neighbor, we must learn to love.

The Bible says that the Samaritan "was moved with pity." In other words, he had compassion on the man because love caused him to act. He was not a neighbor to the man because someone made him. He was not a neighbor to the man because somebody was watching him and he wanted to make a good impression. He was not a neighbor to the man because he was somebody he knew. He was not even a neighbor to the man for money. He helped him because he was moved by something on the inside — something deeper than a warm, fuzzy feeling; something on the inside that was deeper than a rapid heartbeat and weak knees. He was moved by what the old saints would call "something on the inside working on the outside." And that "something" was a love that was not dependent on emotions. It was a love that the apostle Paul would describe as patient and kind, a love that bears all things, believes all things, hopes all things, and endures all things. It was a love that did not seek its own interests. Nor was it rude or unseemly. It was a love that would never end, because it did not stop at self-made boundaries but pushed beyond them. It was a love that King says, "makes no distinction between friends and enemies; it is directed toward both."[4] Nowhere in Scripture are we commanded to like anybody, but we are commanded to love our neighbors as ourselves.

Once we love, we recognize that we are no longer the center of the universe and that the world does not revolve around us. We are enabled to look beyond ourselves. The Samaritan was obviously traveling somewhere. Like us, he had people to see, places to go, and things to do. Yet he sacrificed his time, realizing that human life is more precious than being on time. He sacrificed his money because he valued persons more than possessions.

We are compelled to ask ourselves — on this rocky, windy, sometimes dangerous Jericho road we call life, to whom can we be a neighbor? One day God, in the form of Jesus, decided to be a neighbor to us. Some of us were on that Jericho road beaten, broken, and bruised. We did not have enough strength to make it on our own. Our enemies walked by on one side like the priest. Our friends passed by on the other side like the Levite. Our families could not save us, and the world didn't care. When Jesus came he raised us by his power and healed us with his touch, and by his Spirit he strengthened us. With his mercy he forgave us. By his grace he blessed us. With his Word he instructed us.

When Jesus came he cleansed our sin-infected wounds, wrapped us in the bandages of his love, and healed us with the oil of his anointing. Then he lifted us on the wings of the Spirit. Jesus decided that our conversion was worth an old rugged cross, that our salvation was worth a spear in his side. He decided that our redemption was worth a reed of vinegar, that our breakthrough was worth Judas' betrayal, and that our deliverance was worth Peter's denial.

God, through Jesus Christ, decided to be our neighbor first — "He picked me up and turned me around; placed my feet on solid ground." God decided to be our neighbor first — "Amazing grace, how sweet the sound that saved a wretch like me." God decided to be our neighbor first — "I don't know why Jesus loves me. I don't know why he even cares. I don't why he would sacrifice his life. Oh, but I'm glad, so glad, he did."[5]

So you who have received the love of God, you who have ears to hear God's Word: Be a neighbor. Be a neighbor. Be a neighbor. "And then we will be able to move from the bleak and desolate midnight of man's inhumanity to man to the bright and glittering daybreak of freedom and justice."[6]

Notes

1. Martin Luther King Jr., *A Testament of Hope: The Essential Writings and Speeches of Martin Luther King, Jr.* (San Francisco: HarperSanFrancisco, 1991).

2. Ibid., 122.

3. Cain Hope Felder, ed., *The Original African Heritage Study Bible* (Nashville: James C. Winston, 1993), 1499, n. 25.

4. King, *Testament of Hope*, 19.

5. Andre Crouch, "I Don't Know Why Jesus Loves Me."

6. King, *Testament of Hope*, 15.

17

What Did You Leave Behind?

John 4:4–30

Raquel Annette St. Clair

Have you ever met a pack rat, a person who cannot seem to throw anything away, who has so much old stuff that he or she is running out of room for new stuff? Pack rats have clothes that have already been in style twice. They have so many cards, letters, notes, and random pieces of paper that if it they were all recycled, we would never have to kill another tree. They have so much junk — things that take up space but do not work, like TVs with no picture, radios that get only one station, toys that no one can play with because pieces are missing, three-legged chairs and two-legged tables — that there is hardly any room to sit or stand.

Pack rats are not collectors of specific items like stamps, coins, trains, or dolls. No, they are keepers. They keep everything that comes their way, horde whatever they can hold on to, and save everything they can store. And they can store a whole lot of stuff!

It is easy to spot pack rats. A simple visit to their home or a quick ride in their car will present some telltale signs. Or if you ever made the mistake of throwing something of theirs away that you thought was junk and encountered their wrath, you have met a pack rat.

But there is another type of pack rat that is not so easy to spot — emotional pack rats. We store up feelings, emotions, and attitudes that we refuse to throw away. We have anger that may have been justified at one time, but now it is twenty years later and we have stored up that anger like an old dress that we have just been waiting for the right occasion to display again.

We have so much bitterness, hostility, and negativity that even the people who love us do not like to be around us. We are filled with junk. Emotional baggage, deep-rooted stuff, takes up all of the available space in our hearts and minds but does not help us move forward. We are like the TV with no picture. When people look at us, all they see is a blank screen with no new idea or spark of life. We are like the radio with only one station. We sing the same old, tired sob song. Everybody knows the words — "how we've been 'buked and scorned; talked about as sure as you're born," and even though we aren't tired of singing it, people sure are tired of listening to it. We are like the toys that no one can play with because the pieces are missing. No one can fun with us anymore because we are missing our joy, our smile, our laughter, and our sense of humor. We are like a three-legged chair. Propped up against a wall, we can stand straight. But if anyone leans on us, we will all end up on the floor.

We have so much old stuff that there is no room for anything new. So many old complaints that there is no room for new compliments. So much old bitterness that there is no room for new blessings. So much old unforgiveness that there is no more room for new understanding. So many old attitudes that there is no more room for original action. We have let the past block us. We cannot form any new relationships, friendships, plans, or goals because we cannot get over what he said, she did, or our own failures. And this is not a unique situation. As a matter of fact, it was some of the same stuff the Samaritan woman in John 4:4–30 was dealing with.

Jesus was sitting at the well at about noon when the Samaritan woman came with her water jar. The gospel writer includes the specific time of day because it is an unusual time for a woman to be at the well getting water. It is customary in desert climates for the women to draw water in the cool of the day during the evening hours.

Not only is the Samaritan woman at the well at an unusual time, she is also alone. Women would usually go to the well together so that they might assist one another and serve as protection against strangers and aggressors. Genesis 24:11 states it clearly. When Isaac and his father's servant went to find Isaac a wife, they arrived at a certain well "toward evening, the time when women go out to draw water." Here is this lone woman, in the heat of the day, going to the well to draw water. She knows when the other women are usually there, yet she chooses a time to go when it is most unlikely that she will encounter anyone.

This woman of African descent is truly an alienated person. She is separated from the Jews, her geographic neighbors. The Samaritans occupied the northern portion of Palestine and the Jews the southern portion. The Samaritan woman even points to a common religious and cultural heritage, one that Jesus does not dispute, when she says, "Our ancestors worshiped on this mountain" (John 4:20). For the district of Samaria was settled by the Joseph tribes, Ephraim and Manasseh.[1] These two children, through whom the tribes descended, were the sons of Joseph and his Egyptian (African) wife Asenath. Jeremiah 31:5–6 also links the region of Samaria with the tribe of Ephraim:

> Again you shall plant vineyards
>   on the mountains of Samaria;
> the planters shall plant,
>   and shall enjoy the fruit.
> For there shall be a day when sentinels will call
>   in the hill country of Ephraim,
> "Come let us go up to Zion,
>   to the LORD our God."

When Samaria, the capital city of Israel, was captured in 721 B.C. by the Assyrians, the paganization of the people began (see 2 Kings 17).[2] Genesis, however, traces a common ancestry between the Assyrians and Israel. Noah's son, Ham (the father of African peoples) begat Cush (Ethiopia). Cush begat Nimrod, the mighty hunter and founder of the Assyrian cities of Nineveh, Rehoboth-ir and Calah (Genesis 10:1–11). The Samaritan woman's initial question and John's commentary, however, reveal plainly the schism between these two peoples: " 'How is that you, a Jew, ask a drink of me, a woman of Samaria?' (Jews do not share things in common with Samaritans)" (John 4:9).

Not only is this woman separated from her Jewish counterparts, she is also alienated from her own people. In all of our discussion and resistance to outside subjugation and dehumanization that alienates us from society at large, let us not overlook or excuse ourselves from allowing divisions that separate us from the members of our communities of faith, culture, and ethnicity.

Here comes this woman. She knows that the Jews do not want any part of her. The fact that she is alone suggests that neither does her own community. Unfortunately, some of us can identify with her story. She has had five husbands. Unlike Elizabeth Taylor, her marriages do not make her popular with the men or the women. Remember that in her society the right of divorce belonged only to men. That means that five times she walked down the aisle, and five times they walked out the door. Five times she said, "I do," and five times they said, "I don't." Five times she tried her best, and five times they let her know her best was not good enough. And even if the marriages did not end in divorce, the thought of five men dying on the same wife makes people uncomfortable. And now she has number six, but he isn't really number six, because he isn't really her husband.

This Samaritan woman has been neglected and rejected. She has no alimony, no child support, and no just divorce settlement. She is hurt and humiliated, but she is managing. She is still able to take care of the basics. She does go to the well after all, just like we go to church and work and school. But she is alone. Perhaps that is because of what she said or what he did or her own sense of failure. Perhaps it is because of all of the stuff she's still packin'. And there sits Jesus.

We know that this is going to be a turning point. No one who really meets Jesus leaves the same way. Lepers met Jesus and left clean. Lame people met Jesus and left walking. Blind people met

Jesus and left seeing. Mute people met Jesus and left talking. Mentally ill people met Jesus and left sane. Hungry people met Jesus and left full. Dead people met Jesus and left living. I know some hurting people who met Jesus and left happy. I know some confused people who met Jesus and left understanding. I know some broken people who met Jesus and left feeling built up. And I know some sinful people who met Jesus and left saved. So there is no reason to believe that the Samaritan woman is going to leave the same after this encounter.

But everyone Jesus changed had to leave something behind. The lepers had to leave their social isolation. The lame man had to leave behind sitting on his mat. The blind beggar had to leave behind his cloak. The mute man had to leave behind his stammering tongue. The Gerasene demoniac had to leave behind Legion. The hungry had to leave behind their hunger. The dead had to leave behind their graves. The hurting people had to leave behind their hurt. The broken people had to leave behind their brokenness. The sinful people had to leave behind their sin. And the Samaritan woman left behind her water jar.

It seems obvious that we would have to leave behind some old stuff in order to move forward. But are we willing to leave it behind to experience a change? The Samaritan woman left her water jar. She got so caught up in God's purpose that she forgot her original plan. The woman came for some ordinary liquid and left with extraordinary life. She came to fill up a jar, but Jesus filled her up instead. She came as a water carrier, but she left as a witness.

If we are ever going to truly follow God, we have to leave behind our plans and follow God's purpose. We may be seeking a message, but God is trying to give us a miracle. We may be in church looking for a spouse, but God is trying to give us salvation. We may be planning revenge, but God is preparing us for reconciliation.

The Samaritan woman had not only to leave behind her plan, she had to leave behind her mode of operation and implement God's method. "If we keep on doing what we have always done, we will keep on getting what we already got." The woman kept on going to the well when no one was there and kept on being isolated from her people. In other words, if we continue spending money in the same old reckless ways, we will remain broke. If we continue treating people in the same hateful ways, we will stay friendless. If we continue praying the same old prayer and worship the same old way — with ritual but without the Spirit — we will remain powerless, because God is trying to do something new in us, for us, and through us. Jesus gave that woman new water so she would not just *have* something different, but so she could *do* something different.

God does not make us into a new creation so that we can be the same old creatures of habit. God does not bless us in new ways so that we can utter the same old complaints. God does not answer our prayers in new ways so that we can keep the same old doubts. God does not mature us in new ways so that we can keep the same old ministries, putting on the same old programs with same old people. God does not give us new power to deal with the same old pettiness and problems. No, God desires to take us to new levels in service, giving, witnessing, and living. And if we would leave some of that old stuff behind us, we could receive a new vision of who God is and who we are in him.

The Samaritan woman learned that Jesus was not just a man and not just a Jew. He was not just somebody else's Messiah; he was her Messiah too. She said, "Come and see a man who told *me* everything I have ever done" (John 4:29, my emphasis). Jesus must be the Messiah. Not because of what I've read. Not because of what they told me. But because of my own life-changing, mind-transforming, soul-satisfying experience with Jesus. I don't know about you and your experience with the Master, but he healed *me*. He saved *me*. He forgave *me*. He blessed *me*. He loves *me*. He made a way for *me*.

The woman who left the well was not the same woman who went to the well. Jesus gave her a new vision of who she was so that she could face the people from whom she had been separated. She wasn't just a divorcée. She wasn't just a woman who had multiple husbands and boyfriends. She was a child of God.

She was the recipient of living water. She was an overcomer. And she had a new song:

> Blessed assurance, Jesus is mine.
> O what a foretaste of glory divine.
> Heir of salvation, purchase of God.
> Born of his Spirit, washed in his blood.
> This is my story, this is my song,
> Praising my Savior all the day long.
> This is my story, this is my song,
> Praising my Savior all the day long.[3]

Notes

1. J. D. Purvis, "Samaria, City of," in *Harper's Bible Dictionary*, James L. Mays, ed. (San Francisco: HarperSanFrancisco, 1971), 895–96.

2. J. D. Purvis, "Samaria, District of," in *Harper's Bible Dictionary*, James L. Mays, ed. (San Francisco: HarperSanFrancisco, 1971), 896–97.

3. Fanny J. Crosby, "Blessed Assurance."

18

Saving the One

Acts 8:26–29

William D. Watley

O ne is worth saving. No life devoted to saving and redeeming, teaching and guiding, lifting and inspiring one person should ever be considered wasted or insignificant. This is a truth we must never forget as we invest our time and energy in individuals about whom we care or those whose lives cross ours in the line of duty or by divine providence. This is a truth we must not forget as many of us measure the significance of our contributions with others who have accomplished much more and have achieved broader recognition and visibility. We praise God for the Martin Luthers and Martin Luther Kings, the John Wesleys and Joan of Arcs, the Mary McCleod-Bethunes and Eleanor Roosevelts, the William Shakespeares and Charles Drews, the Mahatma Gandhis and Mother Teresas of history. These are persons whose lives and talents, beliefs and commitments, have changed history. I imagine that knowing that one is a mover and shaker of one's profession or of history can bestow a very gratifying as well as humbling sense of achievement. Most of us, however, will not reach the level of national prominence or global influence. Most of us will not be recognized by our peers for meritorious achievements in our professions.

The contributions of most of our lives will be more easily measured, and our sphere of influence will be much smaller. Rather than being superstars who stand out as the focus of attention, most of us will be part of the background crowd whose voices are not distinct and whose faces are nondescript. Rather than changing history, most of us will spend our lives influencing individuals in our families, our circle of friends, our associates on our jobs, and members of our church. However, we must never underestimate the importance of touching, guiding, and caring for the lives of others. We may not receive much glory or fame from our efforts, but one person is worth saving. Any time an individual calls our name blessed and praises God because we have passed his or her way, our living has not been in vain.

The importance of saving one person is demonstrated in today's text. The angel of the Lord came to Philip and said, "Get up and go toward the south to the road that goes down from Jerusalem to Gaza." This may have seemed like a strange command to Philip, for he was in the midst of a very successful revival in a city of Samaria. Each service was well attended, the sick were healed, demons were cast out, and many people received the liberating word of the gospel. The whole city was stirred by the power of the Holy Spirit that was at work in Philip's ministry. News of Philip's phenomenal success in this Samaritan city reached Jerusalem, and Peter and John, the two major leaders among the apostles went to see what was happening.

It was appropriate that John was named as a representative, because during Jesus' lifetime, he and his brother, James, had visited some of the villages of Samaria. They had not been hospitably received, and James and John had asked the Lord if they should call down fire from heaven to consume those who had rejected them. Our Lord informed them that while they had been blessed with the right power, they had the wrong spirit. For the Son of Man came not to destroy life, but to save life. Let us never forget that power without the right spirit can be dangerous, and opportunity without the right attitude can be nonproductive. If we are to use power the right way, and make rightful and proper use of our opportunities, then we must have the right spirit.

Fortunately, John's temper and frustration were restrained to observe what the Holy Spirit had wrought through the ministry of someone else. Let us be careful about calling a situation

hopeless or a person worthless because we have not been able
to make any progress in a situation. Sometimes another person
with a different approach, who comes at a different time, is able
to· do what we cannot. It takes a big person to admit that another has succeeded where we could not. Most of us tend to
downplay the success of another by talking about how hard it
was for us and how easy it was for him or her. However, a big
person with the right spirit, despite the personal pain or embarrassment that may be involved, is able to say, "I did my best, but
I just couldn't pull the load. Another person succeeded where
I couldn't. Praise God." One plants, another waters, but God
gives the increase.

Peter and John laid hands on the Samaritan converts, and
the Holy Spirit came upon them. The Samaritan revival must
have been a personally gratifying experience for Philip. First, the
word that he gave was well received. Second, he had succeeded
in a place others found difficult. Third, his work had been noted
by two of the most powerful leaders of the early church. Fourth,
the Holy Spirit had validated the genuineness of the faith of the
Samaritan converts. Philip's ministry was truly being blessed in
Samaria. Why then would the angel of the Lord, in the midst
of all that was happening, instruct Philip to leave the populous
region where he was and journey south toward Gaza?

Irrespective of the strangeness of the command, Philip
obeyed. This is the meaning of faith. When God acts in ways
that seem strange, when we receive messages that don't make
sense, still we trust and obey. Faith means that we trust and
obey even when we don't completely comprehend the message,
because we believe in the messenger. Faith is preparing to build
on the strength of a vision because we trust the Spirit who
gave it. Faith is walking forward when the way is not clear and
the full plan has not been revealed, because the God whom we
serve has never led us wrong.

Philip obeyed the angel, and as he walked the lonely desert
road that led toward Gaza, he saw an Ethiopian eunuch, a minister of Candace, queen of the Ethiopians, who was in charge
of all her treasure. He had come to Jerusalem to worship and

was returning home in a chariot. He was reading the prophet Isaiah when the Spirit told Philip to join him. Philip had been commanded by an angel to leave a populous city of Samaria to go down the desert road toward Gaza so that he could meet an Ethiopian. Ethiopia in this passage was not the nation state that we know today, but the Sudan. The person to whom Philip was directed was an African of ebon hue; he was of a different race than Philip.

Let us note the kind of African the man was. He was called a eunuch, a term that normally indicates a person who has been castrated. The term could also be used, however, to refer to a court official. This may be the use of the term in this context when one considers the description of him. He is described as a minister of Candace, queen of the Ethiopians, in charge of all her treasure. Candace was the term applied to all queens of Ethiopia, just as the kings of Egypt were called pharaohs and the emperors of Rome were called Caesar. This man was a high state official of some means. Notice that he was riding in a chariot while Philip was walking. The fact that he was reading indicates that he was not even driving himself but probably had a servant or his own private charioteer. He was not under a fig tree as was Nathanael, or collecting taxes as was Matthew, or fishing as was Peter. He was reading, which says that he was a literate black man.

Now let us note what the eunuch was reading — the prophet Isaiah. The Scriptures were written in either Hebrew or in Greek versions known as the Septuagint. Neither of these languages was his native tongue. Thus, this African was not only literate, he was multilingual. He was the social and political superior of Philip.

When one remembers that at that time the early church was made up of primarily ordinary working and poor people, like many of us, the African was probably a cut above the average member of the early church. One of the myths that racists have told us, that too many of us have believed, is that we were cannibals and brutes cursed of God before whites started "civilizing" us. The Bible, however, is a direct refutation of these myths. It presents a different picture of the faith, cultures, and history of black people. We were not cursed of God; rather, God heard the prayer of the African woman Hagar when she cried to him in the wilderness. After she had been expelled from Abraham's household by a jealous and insecure Sarah, the angel of the Lord told Hagar that her son would be the father of a strong and independent people whom no one could tame.

Lest we forget, the Egyptians, who were North Africans, were a civilized people. The Israelites during the period of Egyptian power were wandering nomads. The queen of Sheba, who visited Solomon, was not only a woman of beauty, grace, and charm, but also wealth, power, and wisdom. She came to Solomon seeking wisdom, not courtship. Whatever present Solomon gave her, she reciprocated with equal quality. Song of Solomon 1:5 of the Revised Standard Version states, "I am black but comely." The Jerusalem Bible translates that phrase, "I am black but lovely." The Living Bible states, "I am dark but beautiful, O girls of Jerusalem, tanned as the dark tents of Kedar." Lest we forget, when Jesus stumbled with the cross, Simon of Cyrene, in Africa, was conscripted to carry it for him, and his family became leaders in the early church.

In our text, the Spirit directs Philip to an African statesman. I don't know how Philip felt about leaving populous Samaria to meet an African coming from Jerusalem, but such were the instructions of the Holy Spirit. Most of the time those to whom we are called upon to minister are not the persons we would ordinarily choose. Maybe that's why the Spirit directs us to them, because we would not choose them on our own. We may think that they are too far above us or too far beneath us. We may not think that they are interested in spiritual things and will not be responsive to the Word of the Lord. But I have discovered that you cannot judge a person's spirituality by their looks and not even by their jobs. Sometimes saints must earn their living by working in the employment of Caesar. However, even though they may be employed by Caesar, they know in what they have believed.

People may have looked at this fine Ethiopian statesman, and based upon his race or position, judged him to be a worldly man; but as Philip discovered, he was not. When Philip approached him, he heard him reading a familiar passage from Isaiah:

> "Like a sheep he was led to the slaughter,
>   and like a lamb silent before its shearer,
>   so he does not open his mouth.
> In his humiliation justice was denied him.
>   Who can describe his generation?
>   For his life is taken away from the earth." (Acts 8:32–33)

The Ethiopian asked Philip, "About whom, may I ask you, does the prophet say this, about himself or about someone else?" Philip started with the Isaiah passage and began telling him the good news of Jesus, who was born in a rugged grotto, lived the life of a rugged carpenter, until he was baptized by the rugged John the Baptist. He was tempted in the rugged wilderness and called twelve rugged followers to be his disciples. He worked among rugged ordinary people and was subjected to a rugged mock trial. He was handed over to a rugged mob. He told him about a Savior who could have called legions of angels to his defense but instead chose to suffer and die on a rugged cross on a rugged hill called Calvary, under a rugged sky whose sun refused to shine, between two rugged thieves, and among rugged soldiers who gambled for his robe, the only piece of property he owned. A rugged crown of thorns was placed upon his head. He was cursed, mocked, and spat upon by rugged onlookers. And in the end a soldier pierced him with a rugged spear. He endured all of this that rugged sinners in the hands of a rugged Satan and under the sentence of a rugged death might become the children of God. Philip told the Ethiopian about a Savior who refused to melt the rugged mess of the world with more ruggedness, but with righteousness. But the righteousness of a crucified Jesus was more powerful than the ruggedness of this world, because it transformed an old rugged cross into a symbol of righteousness. That's why some two thousand years later we are able to sing, "At the cross, at the cross, where I first saw the light and the burden of my heart rolled away. It was there by faith I received my sight, and now I am happy all the day."

The same choice that faced Jesus is the same choice that we face — ruggedness or righteousness. When we hear lies floating around about us, we have a choice as to how we will deal with them — through the ruggedness of more lies or the righteousness of a life that lives down a lie. Do we handle difficult people, difficult situations, and difficult problems with ruggedness or righteousness? Do we handle conflict with ruggedness or righteousness? When the enemies of Jesus came to arrest him in the Garden of Gethsemane, Peter withdrew his sword to defend the Master. But Jesus told him, "Put your sword back into your sheath, for those who live ruggedly, will die ruggedly."

Philip told the Ethiopian that Jesus could do for an individual what he had done with the cross. He could transform ruggedness into righteousness. Then Philip told the Ethiopian that part of the story that his soul longed to hear. He, the Ethiopian, could be saved from ruggedness to righteousness. All he had to do was repent of his sins, believe in the power of the Lord Jesus Christ, and receive the baptism of the Holy Spirit, and he could be righteous.

The Ethiopian knew all about ruggedness and righteousness. He knew that what the world needed was not more ruggedness but more righteousness. The world already had enough people who knew how to return one curse word with another, one frown with another, one mean act and unkind deed with another. What the world needs, what our homes need, what our young people need, what the church needs are a few more examples of transforming righteousness. Thus, when they reached a stream of water, the Ethiopian asked Philip if anything prevented him from being baptized. The Ethiopian and Philip, the African and the Palestinian, the preacher and the statesman, walked into the water, and Philip baptized him. After the Ethiopian's baptism, the Spirit caught up Philip and took him to Azotus, and from there he went into Caesarea preaching the gospel. The Ethiopian went rejoicing on his way.

Philip had no other encounter on the road to Gaza. The Lord evidently had taken Philip away from Samaria and placed him out on the lonely road to Gaza for just one person. One is worth saving. When Jesus passed through Jericho, he heard the voice of blind Bartimaeus crying for mercy over the shouts of the crowds and healed him. One is worth saving. He took the time to call Zacchaeus out of a tree in the midst of a crowd. One is worth saving. In the press of a crowd, Jesus felt the touch of a woman with an issue of blood and healed her. One is worth saving. He told the story of a good shepherd who leaves ninety-nine sheep to look for the one who is lost. One is worth saving. Even when Jesus was on the cross dying for the sins of the whole world, he didn't forget about the one thief who asked for mercy. Jesus told him, "This day you shall be with me in Paradise." One is worth saving. Even after Jesus ascended into heaven, he appeared one day on the Damascus Road to a religious bigot whose name was Saul and put him on a street called Straight. One is worth saving.

Mothers and fathers, keep on praying — that problem child is worth saving. Teachers, keep on teaching — that difficult student is worth saving. Christians, keep on witnessing — that friend, neighbor, or coworker who has not yielded to the Lord is worth saving. Husbands and wives, keep on trying — that companion whose life is controlled by the adversary is worth saving. Doctors, keep on working — that sick patient who won't follow your instructions is worth saving. Lawyers, keep on pleading your case — your client is still God's child no matter what he or she has done and is worth saving. Preachers keep on preaching — that unredeemed sinner and stubborn church member are worth saving.